The Open Couple and
An Ordinary Day

The Open Couple and *An Ordinary Day* deal with the fate of women in a society in which both the social system in which they live and its dominant ideology are shaped by men. In **The Open Couple** Antonia is trying to cope with her philandering husband. In the past, she has threatened to commit suicide with each new mistress but when she changes her tactics and decides to live by his rules, she finds their 'open' marriage is a hypocritical sham. In **An Ordinary Day** Julia is making a video for her husband to see after she has killed herself, but she is interrupted by telephone calls from other women mistaking her for a psychoanalyst. Her reluctant advice to them illuminates her own problems.

The Open Couple was first performed in 1983 in Trieste and **An Ordinary Day** was first performed in 1986 in Milan.

DARIO FO was born in 1926 in Lombardy. He began working in the theatre in 1951 as a comic and mime. Together with Franca Rame, he was highly successful as actor, director and writer of satirical comedies for the conventional theatre. In the Sixties they abandoned it; Fo began to write for a wider audience in factories and workers' clubs and produced work which was not only an important political intervention in Italy but has been internationally acclaimed. In 1970 Fo and Rame founded the theatrical collective, La Comune, in Milan. His work – and the work of Franca Rame – has been performed in England with great success: *Can't Pay? Won't Pay!* (Half Moon Theatre and Criterion Theatre, London, 1981); *Accidental Death of an Anarchist* (Half Moon Theatre and Wyndham's Theatre, London, 1980); *Female Parts* by Franca Rame (National Theatre, London, 1981); *Mistero Buffo* (Riverside Theatre, London, 1983); *Trumpets and Raspberries* (Palace Theatre, Watford; Phoenix Theatre, London, 1984); *Archangels Don't Play Pinball* (Bristol Old Vic, 1986) and *Elizabeth* (Half Moon Theatre, London, 1986). *An Ordinary Day* has also been translated by Ed Emery as *A Day Like Any Other*.

DARIO FO
and
FRANCA RAME

The Open Couple

translated by STUART HOOD

An Ordinary Day

translated by JOE FARRELL

Introduced by STUART HOOD

Methuen Drama

METHUEN MODERN PLAYS

First published in Great Britain in 1990 by Methuen Drama,
Michelin House, 81 Fulham Road, London SW3 6RB.

The Open Couple translation copyright © 1985, 1990 Stuart Hood
Original Italian edition *Coppia Aperta, Quasi Spalancata* copyright
© 1983, Dario Fo/Franca Rame
An Ordinary Day translation copyright © 1990 Joe Farrell
Original Italian edition Un Giornata, Qualumque copyright © 1983
Dario Fo/Franca Rame
Introduction copyright © 1990 Methuen Drama
The authors have asserted their moral rights.

A CIP catalogue record for this book is available from the British
Library.

ISBN 0-413-64050-7

The photograph on the front cover is from *The Open Couple* with
Franca Rame and Giorgio Biavati © Zamborlini
The photograph of Franca Rame and Dario Fo on the back cover is
© Max Whittaker

Printed and bound in Great Britain
by Cox & Wyman Ltd, Cardiff Road, Reading

Contents

INTRODUCTION
The Theatre of Dario Fo and Franca Rame

The son of a railway worker, Dario Fo was born in 1926 near the Lago Maggiore in Northern Italy. He grew up in a village community that included glass-blowers and smugglers, where there was a strong tradition of popular narrative – much of it humorously subversive of authority – fed by travelling story-tellers and puppeteers. Gifted artistically, he studied architecture at Milan at the art-school attached to the Brera Gallery; but the theatre drew him strongly – first as a set-designer and then as a performer. His career began in revue which was the spectacular escapist entertainment of post-war Italy with girls and comics (some very brilliant like Totò, whom Fo greatly admired) and glamorous *chanteuses*. It was a genre favoured by politicians of the ruling Christian Democrat party; girls' legs were preferable to the social preoccupations of contemporary Italian cinema. In revue Fo began to make his mark as an extraordinarily original comic and mime. On radio he built a reputation with his monologues as a Poer Nano – the poor simpleton who, in telling Bible stories, for example, gets things wrong, preferring Cain to the insufferable prig, Abel. In 1954 he married Franca Rame, a striking and talented actress, who came from a family of travelling players and had made her first stage appearance when she was eight days old. Together they embarked on a highly successful series of productions.

In the fifties the right-wing clerical Christian Democrat government had imposed a tight censorship on film, theatre and broadcasting. Fo took advantage of a slight relaxation in censorship to mount an 'anti-revue', *Il dito nell'occhio* (One in the Eye). His aim was clear – to attack those myths in Italian life which, as he said, 'Fascism had imposed and Christian Democracy had preserved.' *Il dito nell'occhio* was 'one in the eye' for official versions of history. Presented at the Piccolo Teatro in Milan it was an immense success to which the participation of the great French mime, Jacques Lecoq, from whom Fo learned much, was an important contribution. *Il dito nell'occhio* was the first in a series of pieces which drew on French farce, on the traditional sketches of the Rame family, and on the traditions of the circus. This mixture of spectacle, mime and social comment was highly successful but made the authorities nervous; the police were frequently present at performances, following the scripts with pocket torches to ensure that there were no departures from the officially approved text. Fo grew in stature and virtuosity as actor and comic, exploiting his extraordinary range of gesture, movement and facial expression, his variety of voices and accents, and his skill as a story-teller. It was the misfortune of Italian cinema that it was unable to exploit his talents. There were difficulties in finding suitable scripts and, on set, his vitality and spontaneity were denied the space and freedom that the theatre provided. But what Fo did take away from film was an understanding of how montage gave pace to narrative.

In 1959 the Dario Fo–Franca Rame company was invited to open a season at the Odeon Theatre in Milan. The piece they chose was *Gli arcangeli non giocano a flipper* (Archangels Don't Play Pinball), written, directed and designed by Fo. It was unusual in that it dealt critically with certain ludicrous aspects of Italian society. The middle-class audience were astonished by its rhythms and technique and delighted by Fo in the leading role – that of a wise simpleton, who looks back to Poer Nano and forward to a series of similar clowns in later work. Fo and Rame were now securely established both as actors and as personalities in the public eye. Their success in conventional theatre was confirmed by a series of pieces which exploited a mixture of comedy, music and farcical plots in which Fo would, for instance, double as an absent-minded priest and a bandit. The social references were there – Fo and Rame were now both close to the Communist Party and acutely aware of the political tensions in society – and the public readily picked them up. In a period which saw widespread industrial unrest culminating in the general strike of 1960 their material caused the authorities in Milan to threaten to ban performances.

Italian television had been for many years a fief of the Christian Democrats. Programme control was strict: a young woman given to wearing tight sweaters who looked like winning a popular quiz show had to be eliminated on moral grounds. But when in 1962 the centre-left of the Christian Democrats became dominant there was some relaxation of censorship. It was in these circumstances that the Fo–Rame team was invited to appear on the most popular TV show, *Canzonissima*, which, as its name suggests, featured heart-throb singers along with variety acts. Into this show the Fo's proceeded to inject their own variety of subversive humour – such as a sketch in which a worker whose aunt has fallen into a mincing-machine, which cannot be stopped for that would interrupt production, piously takes her home as tinned meat. The reaction of the political authorities and of the right-wing press was to call for censorship, duly imposed by the obedient functionaries of Italian television – all of them political appointees. There was a tussle of wills at the end of which the Fo's walked out of the show. The scandal was immense. There were parliamentary questions; threats of law-suits on both sides. Fo had public opinion solidly behind him. He had, he said, tried to look behind the facade of the 'economic miracle', to question the view that 'we were all one big family now' and to show how exploitation had increased and scandals flourished. By subverting *Canzonissima* from within he had established himself with a huge popular audience.

During this period Fo had become interested in material set in or drawn from the Middle Ages. He had begun 'to look at the present with the instruments of history and culture in order to judge it better'. He invited the public to use these instruments by writing an ambiguous piece, *Isabella, tre caravelle e un cacciaballe* (Isabella, Three Caravels and a Wild-Goose Chaser), in which Columbus – that schoolbook hero – is portrayed as the upwards striving intellectual who loses out in the game of high politics. It was a period when Brecht's *Galileo* was playing with great success in Milan and the theatre was a subject of intense debate in the intellectual and political ferment leading up to the unrest of 1968. For Fo the most important result was probably his collaboration with a group of left-wing musicians who had become interested in the political potential of popular songs. Their work appealed to him because he was himself 'interested above all in a past attached to the roots of the people . . . and the concept of "the new in the traditional".' They put together a show, built round popular and radical songs, to which Fo contributed his theories on the importance of gesture and the rhythms in the performance of folksong; it marked an important step in his development.

In 1967 he put on his last production for the bourgeois theatre, *La signora non è da buttare* (The Lady's Not For Discarding), in which a circus was made the vehicle for an attack on the United States and capitalist society in general. It again attracted the attention of the authorities. Fo was called to police headquarters in Milan and threatened with arrest for 'offensive lines', not included in the approved version, attacking a head of state – Lyndon Johnson. By now it was becoming 'more and more difficult to act in a theatre where everything down to the subdivision of the seating . . . mirrored the class divisions. The choice for an intellectual', Fo concluded, 'was to leave his gilded ghetto and put himself at the disposal of the movement.'

The company with which the Fo's confronted this task was the cooperative Nuova Scena – an attempt to dispense with the traditional roles in a stage company and to make decision-making collective. It was, Fo said in retrospect, a utopian project in which individual talents and capabilities were sacrificed to egalitarian principles. But whatever the internal difficulties there was no doubt as to the success the company enjoyed with a new public which it sought out in the

working-class estates, in cooperatives and trade union halls, in
factories and workers' clubs. It was a public which knew
nothing of the theatre but which found the political attitudes
the company presented close to its experience of life. Each
performance was followed by a discussion.

Nuova Scena did not last long – it was torn apart by political
arguments, by arguments over the relationship of art to
society and politics, and by questions of organisation. There
were also difficulties with the Communist Party, which often
controlled the premises used and whose officials began to
react negatively to satirical attacks on their bureaucracy, the
inflexibility of the Party line, the intolerance of real
discussion. Before the split came, the company had put on a
Grande pantomima con bandiere e pupazzi medi e piccoli
(Grand Pantomime with Flags and Little and Medium
Puppets), in which Fo used a huge puppet, drawn from the
Sicilian tradition, to represent the state and its continual fight
with the 'dragon' of the working class. But the most important
production was Fo's one-man show *Mistero Buffo*, which was
to become one of his enduring triumphs in Italy and abroad. In
it he drew on the counter-culture of the Middle Ages, on
apocryphal gospel stories, on legend and tales, presenting
episodes in which he played all the roles and used a language
in part invented, in part archaic, in part drawn from the
dialects of Northern Italy. It has been described as 'an
imaginary Esperanto of the poor and disinherited'. In
performing the scenes of which *Mistero Buffo* is composed –
such as the resurrection of Lazarus, the marriage at Cana,
Pope Boniface's encounter with Jesus on the Via Dolorosa
and others – Fo drew on two main traditions: that of the
giullare (inadequately translated into English as 'jester'), the
travelling comic, singer, mime, who in the Middle Ages was
the carrier of a subversive culture; and that of the great clowns
of the Commedia dell'Arte with their use of masks, of dialect
and of *grammelot*, that extraordinary onomatopoeic
rendering of a language – French, say – invented by the
15th-century comedians in which there are accurate sounds
and intonations but few real words, all adding up (with the aid
of highly expressive mime) to intelligible discourse.

When Nuova Scena split in 1970 it came hard on the heels of mounting polemics in the Communist press. Looking back, Franca Rame has admitted that she and Dario Fo were perhaps sectarian and sometimes mistaken but that they had had to break with the Communist cultural organisations if they wished to progress. The result was La Comune, a theatre company with its headquarters in Milan. The Fo's were now politically linked to the new Left, which found the Communist Party too authoritarian, too locked in the mythology of the Resistance, too inflexible and increasingly conservative. In *Morte accidentale di un'anarchico* (Accidental Death of an Anarchist) Fo produced a piece in which his skill at writing farce and his gifts as a clown were put brilliantly at the service of his politics, playing on the tension between the real death of a prisoner and the farcical inventions advanced by the authorities to explain it. It is estimated that in four years the piece was seen by a million people, many of whom took part in fierce debates after the performance. Fo had succeeded in his aim of making of the theatre 'a great machine which makes people laugh at dramatic things . . . In the laughter there remains a sediment of anger.' So no easy catharsis. There followed a period in which Fo was deeply engaged politically – both through his writings and through his involvement with Franca Rame, who was the main mover of the project – in Red Aid, which collected funds and comforts for Italian political prisoners detained in harsh conditions. His writing dealt with the Palestinian struggle, with Chile, with the methods of the Italian police. In the spring of 1973 Franca Rame was kidnapped from her home in Milan by a Fascist gang, gravely assaulted and left bleeding in the street. Fo himself later that year was arrested and held in prison in Sardinia for refusing to allow police to be present at rehearsals. Demonstrations and protests ensured his release. Dario Fo had, as his lawyer said, for years no longer been only an actor but a political figure whom the state powers would use any weapon to silence.

His political flair was evident in the farce *Non si paga, non si paga* (Can't Pay? Won't Pay!) dating from 1974, which deals with the question of civil disobedience. Significantly, the main upholder of law and order is a Communist shop steward, who disapproves of his wife's gesture of rebellion against the rising cost of living – a raid on a supermarket. It was a piece tried out on and altered at the suggestion of popular audiences – a practice Fo has often used. It was the same spirit that inspired his *Storia di una tigre* (Story of a Tiger), an allegorical monologue dating from 1980 – after a trip to China, and based on a Chinese folktale – the moral of which is that, if you have 'tiger' in you, you must never delegate responsibility to others, never expect others to solve your own problems, and above all avoid that unthinking party loyalty which is the enemy of reason and of revolution. In 1981, following on the kidnapping of Aldo Moro came *Clacson, trombette e pernacchi* (Trumpets and Raspberries). In it Fo doubled as Agnelli, the boss of FIAT, and a FIAT shop steward, whose identities become farcically confused. The play mocks the police and their readiness to see terrorists everywhere and the political cynicism which led to Moro's being abandoned to his fate by his fellow-politicians.

It was the last of Fo's major political works in a period when the great political upsurges in Western Europe have died away and consumerism has apparently triumphed. Yet even when he turned to a play about Elizabeth and Essex, *Almost by Chance a Woman: Elizabeth* with a splendid transvestite part for himself as a bawd, it was possible to read in his portrayal of the machinations of Cecil, Elizabeth's spymaster, a reference to the part played by secret services in Italian politics in the Seventies – and, it might be added, in other Western states. In the meantime he has produced for a theatrical festival in Venice a charming Harlequinade, which is an exercise in the techniques of the Commedia dell'Arte, the tradition from which he has drawn much of his inspiration. His latest play, *The Pope and the Witch*, is once more political not merely in its anti-clericalism – his return to Italian television at the end of the Eighties deeply upset the Catholic hierarchy – but in that it deals with the social problem of drugs and the debate as to whether the solution is to be found in police action or in more enlightened policies which address the needs of the addicts and the social conditions that lead to addiction. It is a piece which has found a strong resonance with Italian audiences.

Meanwhile Franca Rame, who has progressively established herself as a political figure and a powerful feminist voice, has produced performances of a number of one-woman plays in collaboration with her husband – monologues usually which are a direct political intervention in a society where the role of women is notably restricted by the Church, the state and male traditions. Like her husband she finds political intervention difficult in a period which she defines as being one of indifference, of cynicism, of alienation – one in which the grand social causes have been replaced by other issues, green issues, issues affecting deprived children, children with congenital defects, issues like those of drugs and AIDS which are indeed political and of almost universal application.

The Open Couple and *An Ordinary Day* deal with the fate of women in a society in which both the social system in which they live and its dominant ideology are shaped by men. From their earliest days women are, Franca Rame argues, brought up to accept as natural certain social phenomena – that marriage is an institution into which the woman enters for life but the man not necessarily so, that a woman ageing must resign herself to her fate but a man (especially if he is a 'great man') may leave her for a much younger partner, that she must endure loneliness, be misunderstood and considered mad when she cries out for help in unacceptable ways.

Like many of the pieces for women there are in these plays elements drawn from personal experience or from that of friends. Thus in *An Ordinary Day* the episode with the burglars was originally a text written by Franca Rame herself – based on a break-in to her sister's flat. It is a text which, as she says, Dario stole.

Like all the pieces in which Franca Rame appears as the principal character, the original ideas and texts are by Dario Fo; but the texts *as performed* have been shaped by Franca Rame who, over the course of time, has made hundreds if not thousands of changes so that the prompt copy is a palimpsest incorporating references to current events, new pieces of dialogue, textual alterations, which have been incorporated as the result of performances and audiences all over Italy.

Franca Rame is perhaps best described as an actor-manager. She travels from city to city with her own team of actors and technicians. After the curtain has come down the team is likely to meet over a meal and discuss the evening's performance; it is a process in which her interventions range from the technicalities of lighting or sound to the nuances of acting and presentation. After one performance of *An Ordinary Day* in Florence she commented that as usual the audience had remained seated at the end; that was because they were acknowledging the truth of the play.

One of the problems faced by a translator – or director – of Dario Fo's work is where to place the action of his plays. Some – like *Accidental Death of an Anarchist* or *Trumpets and Raspberries* – are clearly set in Italy and are based on specific political events there. The danger to be avoided is then, as Fo himself has pointed out, that of having the plays performed by stage Italians with side-burns and black-and-white shoes as stereotypically untrue as stage Irish or stage Scots. The two plays in this volume are not bound to an Italian setting for they reflect the specific form of the oppression of women in certain societies. (In other societies the form would be different.) The translators have therefore taken the liberty of setting them in England and Scotland respectively. Directors in other countries should, they think, feel free to adapt names and topical references in accordance with local circumstances.

STUART HOOD
May 1990

The Open Couple

translated by STUART HOOD

The Open Couple was first performed at the Teatro Communale di Monfalcone, Trieste, on 30 November 1983. Franca Rame and Nicola de Buono were the performers and Dario Fo directed.

Interior of an apartment. A man in his forties is knocking on the door of the bathroom. His face is lit by a spotlight.

MAN: Don't be silly, Antonia. Come out – say something. What are you doing? Listen – maybe you're right, it's my fault – but please come out. Open the door. We'll talk things over – OK? Christ, why do you have to turn everything into a tragedy? Can't we work things out like rational people? (*He looks through the keyhole.*) What are you up to? You're mad and you simply don't care – that's what's wrong with you.

A woman appears at the side of the stage. She is also lit. The rest of the stage is in darkness.

WOMAN: The uncaring madwoman in there – actually it's the bathroom – is me. That other person – the guy who's yelling at me and begging me not to do anything foolish is my husband –

MAN: (*goes on talking as if the woman were in the bathroom*) Antonia, come out, please!

WOMAN: I'm taking a cocktail of pills. Mogadon, Optalidon, Femidol, Veronal, Cibalgina, four Nisidinetritate suppositories – all orally.

MAN: Say something, Antonia.

WOMAN: My husband's already called an ambulance. They'll break down the door.

MAN: The first-aid squad's on its way. They'll knock the door down. Christ – this is the third time.

WOMAN: The thing I can't stand about emergency treatment is having your stomach pumped. That damned tube down your throat – and then the dazed state you're in for days and the embarrassed looks everyone gives you. Making these vague idiotic comments – just to say something. And then, of course, they make me see the psychologist – pardon, the analyst. A prick who sits there looking at you in silence for two hours with his pipe in his mouth and then suddenly says: 'Do cry, please, do cry!'

MAN: Antonia, say something. Give a moan at least. Then at least I'll have an idea of what stage you're at. I'm going now and you won't see me again. (*He bends down to squint through the keyhole.*)

WOMAN: Actually it's not the first time I've wanted to die.

MAN: Antonia! Don't swallow the yellow pills. They're for my asthma!

WOMAN: Another time I tried jumping out of the window. He grabbed me just when I was taking off. (*The woman jumps onto the window-sill which has been brought onto the stage. The man grabs her ankle. The lights come on full.*)

MAN: Please come down. Yes, you're right – I am a bastard but I promise you, it's the last time I'll put you in a situation like this.

WOMAN: Do you think I give a damn? Can't you understand I'm simply not interested in you – in your affairs – in your stupid women?

MAN: You mean – if they'd been intelligent you wouldn't have minded so much? Let's talk it over – on the floor. Come down.

WOMAN: No, I don't give a damn – I'm going to jump.

MAN: No!

WOMAN: Yes!

MAN: I'll break your ankle first.

WOMAN: Ow! (*She steps down from the window. Her husband hands her a crutch.*)

WOMAN: (*to the audience*) And he really did break it, the idiot. A month with my leg in plaster! And everyone asking me: 'Have you been skiing?' God, was I angry. (*Limping, she puts down the crutch and from the drawer of the table or some other piece of furniture, takes out a gun.*)

WOMAN: Another time I tried to shoot myself –

MAN: No, damn it, stop! (*The* MAN *makes a move to stop the* WOMAN.) I haven't got a licence for it. Do you want to get me arrested? (*The* WOMAN *talks to the audience as if not involved in the action.*)

WOMAN: The reason I wanted to die was always the same. He didn't want me any more. He didn't love me any more. And the tragedy erupted every time I found out about my husband's latest affair.

MAN: (*trying to take the gun away from the woman*) Try to be reasonable. With the others it's only a sexual thing – that's all.

WOMAN: Oh yes? and with me it isn't even sex any more.

MAN: But with you it's different. I've a tremendous respect for you.

WOMAN: Well you know what you can do with your respect! (*To the audience.*) Yes, in this sort of situation I always get a tiny bit petty. But it was my husband's thoughtlessness that drove me up the wall. It couldn't go on like that. He hadn't made love to me for ages.

MAN: I don't know why you get a kick out of dragging everything out in public —

WOMAN: Oh, it pisses you off, eh? (*To the audience.*) At first I thought maybe he was – overtired. (*She is about to cross in front of the window. Her husband who is looking out of the window stops her.*)

MAN: Watch! You'll fall out!

WOMAN: No, I won't. There's the stage.

MAN: Yes, but the set ends here.

WOMAN: Right – but I'm a character in a play. I'm telling a story so I step out of character and I can step out of the set. (*To the audience*.) I was saying – I thought maybe he was overtired and then I found out he had an extremely active sex-life with other people – naturally. And when I asked him to explain what had happened to him – 'Why don't you want me any more?' – he would find excuses. (*During the last part of her speech the* MAN *sits on the window-sill with his legs dangling*.)

MAN: I would find excuses?

WOMAN: Yes, you. Once you even tried to lay the blame on politics.

MAN: Me?

WOMAN: Watch out, you'll fall!

MAN: I'm a character in a play, too!

WOMAN: No, you're not. You're on the fourth floor. (*To the audience*.) I was saying that he tried to lay the blame on politics. He trotted out the bits about the political backlash. 'You've got to understand. How can I make love with all that's going on in this country? The unions –'

MAN: I didn't make it up about the backlash. It's a fact. Isn't it true that after the failure of all those struggles we went through we felt a bit frustrated – teetering on the brink. Look about you – what do you see? Cynicism.

WOMAN: Great! Some people get fed up with politics, dump their families and join the Hare Krishna lot – or else they chuck the office and open up a macrobiotic restaurant – and some of them set up whorehouses for their own personal use. And it's all the fault of politics!

MAN: I admit it's a silly kind of hobby – trying to set up as a sexual athlete – But I swear it's different with you. You're the only woman I can't do without. You're the person I love most in all the world – I feel really safe with you – like my mother.

WOMAN: I knew it! Your mother! Thank you very much! You've promoted me. Wives are like civil servants. When they're no use any more they kick them upstairs – make them director of some useless public corporation. Well, I'd rather be demoted to a one-night stand. Thrown on the bed and desired. I'm damn well not interested in being a warm blanket for you. Your huggy! Your mother! But don't you see what a bore you are? How you humiliate me? What am I supposed to be? An old boot you throw onto the rubbish heap? Your mother! You'll see I can find men how and when I like.

MAN *reacts*.

WOMAN: It's no use putting on that ridiculous self-satisfied smile. I'll set up a brothel for you – yes, a brothel opposite where you work. I'll walk up and down on the pavement with a billboard. It'll have on it: 'Now available – the wife of Mr X – special offer – washed and scented. Handsome discounts.' Passed by the Board of Advertisers.

MAN: That's what I like about you – the way you always shit on my moments of honesty – of sincere feeling. I try to open up – to talk –

WOMAN: Then why don't you talk? Talk! Explain yourself. Explain to me what's got into you? All these stories – about bed – bed – bed. As if I didn't have a properly furnished house. (*While she is speaking the man tries to take the gun away*.) And let go of this gun! I swear I won't shoot myself.

MAN: Word of honour?

WOMAN: Word of honour – I won't shoot myself. I don't feel like it any more. (*The MAN lets go*.) I've changed my mind. It's you I'm going to shoot. (*She points the gun at him*.)

MAN: Don't play silly tricks.

WOMAN: I'm not. (*She fires a shot that just misses him*.)

MAN: Have you gone mad? You fired. You just missed me. Look, we're only re-enacting things.

WOMAN: And I'm getting furious all over again just thinking about it.

MAN: Aren't I ever allowed to be a character in a play?

WOMAN: Shut up! Hands up! Face the wall. Stay like that. I'm going to have a word with them – then I'll kill you. (*She turns to the public still pointing the gun at her husband.*) Then one day he counter attacked.

MAN: And what did you do to stop things from falling apart? And when I did something about it and looked for some affection elsewhere – some sort of stimulus – a bit of passion – something different – did you try to understand me?

WOMAN: Something different! (*To the public.*) One day I discovered him – I was there in the house – washed and perfumed – I discovered him in the loo masturbating like a fifteen-year-old – out of hours. That was something different too!

MAN: That's mean! What sort of a kick do you get out of shitting all over me like this? OK, every so often I get into self-gratification. It's healthy. It relaxes me – especially when I'm tense and depressed. Like taking a sauna.

WOMAN: Yes – sauna my – Don't make me say rude things.

MAN: That's right, try not to. There are a lot of men –

WOMAN: (*threatens him with the gun*) Shut up! (*To the audience.*) As I was saying, my husband counter-attacked – the things he came up with! 'We must talk, you and me – we can only save our relationship if we change our cultural attitudes.' He trotted out all the hypocrisy that goes with bourgeois after-dinner talk – the most disgusting moralizing.

MAN: Of course! Faithfulness is a disgusting idea. Uncivilised! The idea of the married couple, of the family, is tied up with the defence of the immense economic benefits the patriarchy gets out of it. What you aren't able to understand is that I'm perfectly capable of having a relationship with another woman and at the same time of being friends with you –

WOMAN: Did you think this all out yourself or did you have an old boys' reunion? I understand. Adultery's out.

Nowadays we behave like modern people – civilised – politically aware. No! No! I can see myself and I won't stand for it. The bell rings. I go to the door. Who is it? Oh, it's my husband. 'Hello – and who is the nice young lady?' 'May I introduce you – this is my wife – my girl-friend.' 'How nice to meet you. Do come in. She's charming. How old are you? Only twenty-five years younger than my husband! That's marvellous. Do feel at home. Supper is ready. I hope you like our house. This is your bedroom. I mean our bedroom – but you're welcome to it. I'll sleep in my son's room. Or maybe it would be better if I went out. You'll feel freer then. I'll go to my sister's. No, don't worry – it's no trouble – somebody will keep me company. There's Norman – he's free too this evening because his wife's going out with – Have a nice supper and good night. Good luck and I hope it's a boy. No, not that – we have two boys already.' (*To the public*.) And him – he can't believe his luck – sees himself in a kind of harem with his ladies getting along together all sweetness and light. There are only two so far – but later who knows? Everyone happy and without a care in the world. (*To her husband*.) Is that what you'd like? But it's not like that! There are attacks of nerves, bouts of anxiety – then they start popping pills and they're off to the analyst and the looney bin. It's no go. Lots have tried and failed.

MAN: Who gives a damn? When others fail and fall flat on their faces that's when we have a real go at it, start from the beginning again.

WOMAN: Invent open marriage from scratch! Get out! (*To the public*.) But in the end he convinced me. To defend our marriage, our friendship, our privacy, our bed has to go public. There's the problem of the children. Oh, the children will understand, said he. To be able to talk, to discuss, argue, give advice to each other we had to make love 'elsewhere'. Incredible as it may seem it was my son, Robert, who gave me the courage to try. (*When she plays the part of the son she takes on the blasé attitude of youth today – when she plays herself she takes on the mannerism of an embarrassed mother*.) 'Mum, that's enough. You two

can't go on like this. You've got to come up with something
else. To begin with you can't go on living like some sort of
extension of Dad's. You've got to have your own life. Dad
goes after women and you – not for revenge but because it's
right, healthy and human – you should find yourself another
man.' 'What are you saying, Robert?' I don't know why but
I put on a funny accent. 'Mum, don't go on like that. Get
yourself a nice man – maybe younger than Dad. Just watch –
I'll help you.' 'But Robert, what sort of a way is this to talk
to your mother? Look, I'm terribly upset – all of a sweat.
How on earth am I supposed – at my age – to start looking
for men?' 'No,' he says, 'all you have to do is let it be known
you're available. Live your own life, Mum. At least try,
Mum!' I couldn't resist that 'Mum' so I tried. First of all I
went off to live by myself, here. I took all the clothes I got
since I was married and threw them away. Then I rushed off
to get a new wardrobe. I bought way-out pants and
ridiculous skirts.

MAN: I see. You turned yourself into a typical modern idiot.

WOMAN: That's right! My husband's idea of elegance is a
woman who gets her clothes at Laura Ashley's. She may be
very elegant but she doesn't have to find herself a boy-friend
– but I do darling! I changed my way of dressing – then my
make-up – purple! I looked horrible. Then my hair – a crazy
cut. Punk! All my hair standing on end. I looked like an ad
for . . . And the way I walked! Because you all know what a
state we get into when our husbands cheat us – when they
don't want us any more. SAD! Ugly! We cry. We get
round-shouldered. Take me for example – before it
happened I had completely forgotten that I had thighs.
Abandoned yes – but I had thighs didn't I? I walked without
the slightest wiggle. Stiff like a board. I clumped along. (*She
takes a few steps*.) Like this. Like an arthritic camel. I kept
looking at the ground – I don't know why – all I ever found
was dog-shit. What a time that was. The incredible thing is
that the moment I forced myself to loosen up a little, to pay
some attention to myself, to return friendly glances – well, I
found what I wanted. They fell into my arms – after a while I

had quite a crisis. First of all because they were almost all younger than me. What were they looking for? A second mother for an oedipal relationship! I fell for it once. There was this chap – but handsome – so handsome – eyes? – he seemed to have more than two – blue they were – and hundreds of teeth! Madly in love. He wept. He rang me up. I lifted the receiver. All I could hear were sobs. I'm – I'm only a mother. One day I said to him: 'OK darling' and made a date – right out in the suburbs – frightened I'd be seen. I actually thought of putting on a false nose. I arrived all churned up – like an idiot. With my heart going TOM TOM. We sit down. Along comes the waiter. 'What will madam have? And your son?' That was it. 'A double whiskey, please – he'll have a lemonade with a straw.' Yes, there were men of my age too – maybe it's my luck – but the ones that came my way were so sad, so beaten, deserted, betrayed by wives and lovers, by their children and grandchildren.

MAN: You mean – you had a terrific time.

WOMAN: Instead – this husband of mine – the moment I gave him the OK – 'Off you go – we're an open couple – make love as much as you like' – You should have seen him!

MAN: Well, yes. It was the effect of that 'open couple'. I didn't feel got at any more by a guilt complex. I was free!

WOMAN: I had a terrific attack of paranoia but he was walking on air. He took off! When we met he used to tell me how he was getting on.

MAN: But, love, forgive me but it was you who always asked me to tell you things – so I told you.

WOMAN: Yes, I'm a masochist. This was when he was having a relation with a woman – a girl of about thirty but terribly intelligent and liberated – left-wing intellectual – you know the type.

MAN: Yes, she was an intellectual – but why do you say it with that contemptuous voice?

WOMAN: Me? Contemptuous of an intellectual? On the contrary, I was honoured to have one in the house. There was only one week that was a bit heavy-going. She had been in New York. Suddenly she didn't speak her own language any more. 'Say, can I have some cawfee,' 'Have a nice day,' 'You're welcome'. It wasn't as if he fell in love with women of 80. Then it would have been understandable. 'Poor boy, he had an unhappy childhood. He needs his granny. Sit her down there with her knitting.' But this girl – he said to me: 'She's not very pretty but she has a lot of charm. When she's sitting down she exudes sexuality – from her ears!'

MAN: That's mean.

WOMAN: She loved him in quite a different way from – not possessively. In fact she had another man and he had a relationship with another woman and she was married to another man who – a daisy-chain of open couples. But what a job. They needed a computer. X has a date with Y on Monday, Y had a date with Z on Tuesday. Such a business! Then of course – he was very active – he was always away from home. He was only ever there to eat. And at the same time he was carrying on with a very pretty young girl – very nice – always eating something. Ice-creams – even in winter. It was a kind of joke for him. She was still at school and he helped her with her homework.

MAN: Yes, it was a kind of game. I really played with that girl.

WOMAN: Oh yes, they played – hide-and-seek under the sheets. He told me.

MAN: I like her because she's crazy, unpredictable, has tantrums, laughs, throws up ice-cream in lumps. She makes me feel young too – and fatherly at the same time.

WOMAN: A boy-father!

MAN: That's cheap!

WOMAN: 'Watch out that she doesn't get pregnant' I told him. 'Of course', he says, 'watch out but I can't be there to keep an eye on her when she goes out with other boys. She doesn't like that.' Isn't that right?

MAN: Yes, but it was only a joke. It's obvious.

WOMAN: (*to the audience*) One day my husband comes to me all embarrassed and says:

MAN: Listen, this is women's stuff – why don't you go with Paula –

WOMAN: That was the ice-cream girl.

MAN: To the gynaecologist and get her fitted with a coil. Maybe you can convince her – she'll go with you – that's for sure.

WOMAN: Yes, of course I'll be mummy little Paula – of course I'll take her to the gynaecologist. Doctor, please fit my husband's girl-friend with a coil.' Let's hope he's got as good a sense of humour as we have. I'll fit you with a coil. In your foreskin!

MAN: (*to the audience*) You see how she reacted. And that's nothing. (*To his wife.*) Go on – tell them what you did!

WOMAN: Yes, I admit I did react. I'd just finished opening a tin of peeled tomatoes – a 5 kilo one. I poured it over his head and pushed the tin down till it came to his chin – like that. He looked like Sir Lancelot ready for the tournament – sponsored by Buitoni. Then I took advantage of his momentary embarrassment and pushed his hand into the toaster. (*She laughs.*) It was on.

MAN: Look – I've still got the marks. I looked like a toasted sandwich. I walked about with lettuce leaves between my fingers so that people wouldn't notice. (*To the audience.*) Then the shouts, the insults – a fine open couple – a democratic one.

WOMAN: Well, what did you expect? I had taken huge steps towards centrifugal sexual freedom – but what a nerve! to want me to play nanny to his baby dolls. I don't know what came over him. He didn't use to be like that. A man possessed. He leapt from one woman to another at the speed of light. I've talked to other women, friends of mine – I did a bit of research. Their husbands are always randy too. It must be a virus – the randicoccus. Even our porter's wife –

he's randy – always looking for it. But the fact is that my husband doesn't only look for it, he finds it. He's got a mania. Like those people who look for mushrooms – only one thing on their minds – always going to the woods and collecting masses of them. And then they pickle them! Or dry them. Only he collects – birds, chicks, pussies. I swear – it's got to be an obsession with me. I've gone mad. I kept seeing the house full of female sex organs – used and thrown away! I go into the bathroom and instead of a cake of soap – 'It's a pussy!' I put on my shoes. 'Help – there's a mouse!' No, it's a pussy. There are young ones, intelligent ones, stupid ones, good and bad ones, huge ones, thin ones and fat ones. How do I keep them alive? I water them. I get the right stuff to keep them alive from the sperm bank where my husband is an honorary member.

MAN: This is too much. I'm not putting up with any more. Just to please a handful of hardline fanatical anti-male feminist friends of yours you're lynching me!

WOMAN: OK, maybe I've exaggerated for effect. A bit.

MAN: A bit! Here I am reduced to a caricature of a guy who collects mushrooms. The classical example of the penis-dominated sex-maniac and absolutely incapable of any feelings – bang-bang, thank you ma'am! But you took good care not to mention that, for example, I go out with a lot of these women just to talk and not necessarily to go to bed.

WOMAN: But it was you that was always talking to me about sex!

MAN: Yes, of course, because I know for sure that if I tell you that between you and me it's mostly a feeling of closeness you'll get even crosser.

WOMAN: Yes. Maybe. I have to admit that every time I told him about my idiotic moralistic block – about how impossible it was to have a relationship with other men – he gave me a push – like a real comrade, a really understanding friend.

MAN: Now you've discovered I'm not the right man for you, make yourself a new life. You must find a nice man – you deserve it! You're an extraordinary woman – intelligent, generous, fascinating.

WOMAN: (*to the audience*) Dynasty! (*To her husband.*) No – please! I can't. I'm all right like this. If you don't want to stay with me, I'd rather be alone – I'm quite calm – believe me. I'm OK here in my own house. I feel good.

MAN: (*to the audience*) And then she would burst out crying and threaten to kill herself.

The WOMAN *jumps up onto the window-sill again clutching the gun.*

Stop! What's got into you now? Be reasonable – don't be an idiot! (*He tries to stop her by catching her skirt which he pulls down to her feet.*)

WOMAN: Don't make me die without a skirt on! I want to die! I can't go on. I'm sorry I keep involving you and putting you through all this. But this time I'm really going to finish things. I'm going to jump and while I'm falling I'll shoot myself.

MAN: No, Antonia! Why don't you try to look at things with a little detachment – behave like a normal person.

WOMAN: (*gets down from the window and turns to the audience*) So the day came when I finally behaved like a normal person. I got a job. I was fed up with being a domestic martyr. Out! I said. So I went out and found a job – an important one. In the morning you leave the house and take your nice bus. You've no idea how many people you know on a bus. No one! But just to see all these people – squashed together. They pick your pocket. You don't feel alone any more. Whereas at home I was as lonely as a dog. Me and the telly. The commercials. (*TV jingle needed here.*) . . . So I went out in the evenings too – to a drug-addiction centre. Meanwhile he – by the way he hadn't stopped coming round my place even with all those great loves of his – noticed that I was getting more relaxed from day to day.

MAN: Well, what surprised me most of all was that you weren't interested any more in the stories of my adventures.

WOMAN: So to make up for it you kept asking me – (*To the audience.*) There was a hail of questions – he wanted to know if I'd made anyone –

MAN: And she always denied it –

WOMAN: I didn't deny it so much as avoid the question as you did to begin with – remember? It was natural reticence. Your husband is your husband after all! (*To the audience.*) But one day I made up my mind – told him everything. (*To her husband.*) You know, darling, maybe I've found 'Mr Right'.

MAN: Oh yes! Who is he?

WOMAN: Said he and stopped breathing just like that.

MAN: (*annoyed*) Naturally – you caught me on the wrong foot. I felt a pang in the stomach and my belly swelled up –

WOMAN: (*to the audience*) Of course – I'd forgotten. My husband has a terrible ailment. Aerofagia nervosa. When he has a strong emotion – I was even worried on our wedding day – his stomach swells up and – prot – prot – prot! That's with me. Prit – prit. With the others he sings.

MAN: Shut up, will you? When you're at it why don't you let them hear it in stereo. POT POT POT. But I swear – deep down I was very happy for you.

WOMAN: Very deep down. So deep there was no sign of it.

MAN: First of all I gave you a hug right away – you've got to admit it – and with passion.

WOMAN: Too much – but let's play the scene for them.

MAN: Yes, we were playing cards. I was banker. (*They sit at the table to play rummy.*)

WOMAN: It's my cue and I say: You know, darling, maybe I've found Mr Right!

MAN: Delighted to hear it. I'm really terribly pleased for you. (*He mixes the cards and ends up by letting them fall.*)

WOMAN: That was the first time he dropped them.

MAN: Mr Right? At last! Who is he, then? What does he do? (*He picks up the cards.*)

WOMAN: I bet you can't guess. To begin with, he's not anyone you know.

MAN: Really? Well, I prefer it that way.

WOMAN: He's a professor – of physics.

MAN: A don! You know, you mustn't be carried away by appearances.

WOMAN: Hold on! He has a chair in the university.

MAN: With tenure! Wow!

WOMAN: And he's doing research on nuclear energy – for the Atomic Energy Commission.

MAN: Nuclear energy! (*He lets the cards fall again.*)

WOMAN: That was the second time.

MAN: Very interesting. So you'll have learned all there is to know about the safety and social advantages of our nuclear power stations. He'll have convinced you the safest place to install a new megawatt nuclear station is up there – at Dounreay.

WOMAN: (*ironically*) I'm sorry to disappoint you but he is opposed to all those nuclear power stations they're putting up. He says they're out of date – built with stuff the Americans discarded – really dangerous junk – and that our rulers are real villains because they've let themselves be corrupted – but above all they're dangerous because they're idiots. Who is this man? One of his colleagues tells me he's indispensable – otherwise they'd have got rid of him long ago.

MAN: Indispensable? He must be very brainy.

WOMAN: Yes, he's a member of Mensa – but he doesn't give himself airs. He's sensitive and intelligent. The things he says – they ought to be preserved for posterity. When he comes out with one of them he sort of looks away and I take out a notebook and write it all down. The other evening he said: 'There's no doubt that the lowest level of intelligence is that of the politicians – but we scientists are close seconds – that was how we thought up Hiroshima together!'

MAN: He certainly sticks his neck out!

WOMAN: He's got guts – nuclear guts – he's politicised – witty – he makes me lose my head – we spend some wonderful days together. Then I found he's been nominated for a Nobel prize. (*She lays her hand on the table*.) Rummy!

MAN: Just imagine – my wife's lover almost a Nobel prizewinner! It's great to find you have a genius in the family. I'm very honoured.

WOMAN: Yes, but last time you weren't so laid back about it. You said it out of the side of your mouth, 'I'm very honoured.'

MAN: I hope you won't mind an indiscreet question – have you ever been together – I mean, have you made love yet?

WOMAN: And when he asked this question this laid-back, liberated husband – the male half of the open couple – had another attack of his ailment. Prot Prot.

MAN: Cut out the details. I got short of breath. But answer my question.

WOMAN: I'd like to be able to say Yes – but it's No!

MAN: (*with ill-concealed satisfaction*) No love-making. Is there something wrong?

WOMAN: No, nothing. I like him a lot – I'd like to very much. But I don't feel like it yet. He was amazing – he understood at once –

MAN: Understood? What did he understand?

WOMAN: That I didn't feel comfortable about it. 'Urania', he said . . .

MAN: Why 'Urania'? Aren't you called Antonia any more?

WOMAN: Yes, but he calls me Urania which is the core element of Plutonium. He's a physicist – do you want him to call me 'darling'? 'Urania,' he said, 'this thing of ours is too important to rush it. We need a breathing-space.' 'Yes,' I added, 'if not there's the risk it will just be a quick fuck and that's all. It happened to me once before – and I felt like an old rag afterwards.'

MAN: When was this quick fuck? You didn't tell me about it.

WOMAN: Well, it was an unimportant relationship – believe me – just a sexual thing that's all.

MAN: Are you sending me up? That's one of my lines.

WOMAN: It's certainly not one of mine – you know that if there's no love I feel empty – sad.

MAN: And who was it made you empty and sad?

WOMAN: Does it matter?

MAN: Yes, it does. I've always told you all about me.

WOMAN: Well, I don't. I'm reserved. Even with the professor I had problems talking about it.

MAN: Ah, so you told him!

WOMAN: Yes, I did. I feel it's right and honest not to hide anything from him. To show him myself as I am.

MAN: While with me you can show yourself as you aren't. (*Changing tone*.) So it's serious with the atomic expert?

WOMAN: Yes, I think so. Why? Would you rather it was a big joke?

MAN: But why? It was me that advised you – told you how to behave. I'm a civilised person too – democratic and understanding. (*He gives a shriek*.) Aaaaah! I'm an idiot. Look at this – I'm sweating all over. I feel like the original example of the male shit.

WOMAN: Ah you see, one has to admit – the open couple has its disadvantages. Rule Number 1: For the open couple to work properly only one part of it has to be open. Because if it's open on both sides then there are terrible draughts.

MAN: You're right. I feel fine so long as I can chuck you over. I use you, discard you, but if anyone dares pick you up – watch out! If some bastard notices that your wife is still attractive – even if she's been abandoned – and wants her and appreciates her – then it gnaws away at you till you go mad. And into the bargain you discover that the bastard who picks her up is more intelligent, has any number of degrees, is witty – democratic!

WOMAN: Don't put yourself down like that.

MAN: Damn it – all that's missing is for him to play the guitar and sing rock.

WOMAN: You know him then?

MAN: Know who?

WOMAN: The professor. You've had me followed.

MAN: Followed! What are you saying?

WOMAN: Then how do you know that he plays the guitar and sings rock music?

MAN: He really does?

WOMAN: Who told you?

MAN: No one. I just came out with it – I guessed. God damn it! a singing atomic scientist! And I've no ear for music. In any case a man his age who tries to sing like X . . .

WOMAN: What do you mean, of his age? He is thirty-eight. Eight years younger than you. And he doesn't copy X – he has a style of his own. He plays the guitar – the piano – the trumpet – can do American slang . . .

MAN: Ah, so he can do American slang. He's a don at Cambridge and an adviser to the Atomic Energy Corporation. I expect he's a Vegan as well.

WOMAN: And he writes music too –

MAN: I was just saying to myself: 'I wonder if he writes music?'

WOMAN: Yes, words and music. He's had a couple of hits. You know the one that goes – 'a woman without a name is like a fish without a bicycle' – the one that what's her name sings.

MAN: He wrote that!

WOMAN: Yes!

MAN: He writes feminist songs. I never could stand male feminists. Specially when they're thirty-eight.

WOMAN: But it's an ironical song – he's sending up trendy feminism. He wrote one and dedicated it to me. I'm a bit shy about it – but you and I – we're very close – if you like I'll try to sing it.

MAN: Why don't you go on being shy?

WOMAN: I'm glad you didn't insist. I'd have felt terribly embarrassed singing a song to my husband that my new man wrote for me. Wait – I've taped it. (*She turns on the tape-machine.*)

> and you were there
> you still hadn't dialled the number
> to put you through to my love
> and you were there – so beautiful
> On the monitor of my thoughts
> you appeared
> with the speed of a telex –
> marvellous interference –
> so lovely
> you blew all my circuits
> you blew all my circuits – oh yeah!

MAN: That's great. But you'd think it had been written by the speaking clock and not an atomic physicist.

WOMAN: You're right. I had not thought about it. I'll tell him the moment I see him.

MAN: When are you seeing him?

WOMAN: In a minute – at lunch.

MAN: At lunch – already?

WOMAN: Yes, we're spending the weekend together. Do you mind? I've only an hour to get ready.

MAN: But damn it, if he's so important to you – if you get on together – why don't you go and live with him?

WOMAN: Not on your life! I'm not going to be an idiot again and set up with a man. I've had enough of that!

MAN: Not even if – it's just a suggestion – I was to propose it myself?

WOMAN: Never! I'm sorry but I've gone through too much. What's up with you? Don't you feel well? You've been biting your nails for the last hour. You're almost down to the knuckles, my darling. Why don't you have a drop of vodka?

MAN: It's disgusting.

WOMAN: Vodka?

MAN: No – vodka's all right. I'm disgusted with myself. But I asked for it – there's nothing I can do about it. It was me that suggested being an open couple and I can't expect you to go back on it just because I'm fed up with the whole thing. You have an absolute right to organise your own life. God, what balls I'm talking. But, tell me, doesn't rock make you want to throw up? You used to say it was stuff for mental defects and psychopaths. The moment you heard that bam-bam-batapang you got a pain in the stomach.

WOMAN: Yes, that's true. It was a classical case of the total rejection of anything new – anything you can't understand.

MAN: I suppose you like it now because it's in. Because you're carrying on like a teenager – and the professor plays it. All this post-modernist stuff. The truth is – he put you on the right path.

WOMAN: Of course – if a woman improves her mind, transforms herself, there has always to be a man behind it – the latest Pygmalion. What an idiotic idea! (*The telephone rings.*)

MAN: If it's one of my girl-friends say I'm not in, I've gone out.

WOMAN: Why?

MAN: Never mind – I just don't feel like talking –

WOMAN: He's holding out on the harem. (*She takes the phone. She is excited.*) Hi, it's you. Why on earth? Am I late? You gave me such a fright. (*To her husband.*) It's him.

MAN: Who?

WOMAN: Oh piss off. (*To the phone.*) Yes, I'm almost ready. You're coming over? Half-an-hour. (*Embarrassed.*) No, of course I'm alone. Absolutely. I'll be waiting. Yes, I do. Yes, so much. All right I'll spell it out. I love you so much. Bye – bye. (*She slams down the receiver. Furiously.*) You could at least not stand there looking at me with these eyes. You made me terribly embarrassed.

MAN: Why did you say you were alone? Was it too much for you to say I was there?

WOMAN: No. Yes! you're right – it was too much.

MAN: I see. So the Brain is jealous.

WOMAN: Jealous? Don't talk bilge. Drink up your vodka and get out.

MAN: Why?

WOMAN: Didn't you hear? He's coming any minute.

MAN: What is this? Are we swopping roles now? The husband who has to clear out so that the lover doesn't find him there! So it's true. He's jealous of me!

WOMAN: He's not jealous. I just don't want you to meet.

MAN: I see – you're afraid I'll sus out that he's not what you've cracked him up to be. That I won't like him: 'Is that all there is to him? What a let-down!'

WOMAN: What I'm really afraid of is that he won't like you – that you'll be the let-down.

MAN: What do you mean?

WOMAN: Well, you see I painted a very flattering portrait of you – I said you were an extraordinarily intelligent man, witty, open-minded, generous –

MAN: I suppose you mean I'm not –

WOMAN: No, for goodness' sake, you have your points – even you have some. But you see – well – I exaggerated a little. It wasn't exactly a true likeness. Of course everyone has their weaknesses. I like you with all your shortcomings. We've known each other for ages. You were my first big love – but now I'm so totally changed people who know me now can't imagine how I lived with you for so long.

MAN: I didn't notice anything. Do you realise how nasty you are being to me? Who do you think you are?

WOMAN: A different woman, darling.

MAN: Yes – but that means you've gone round the bend. You've blown your mind going alone – with these Brains, these intellectual snobs that write rock lyrics. But I don't give a damn for you or for your stupid friends with brains coming out of their ears.

WOMAN: Great! But I thought you'd make a scene. Now please go away. In any case I can't stand that thing you've got round your neck. You look like something out of a Thirties film.

MAN: Shut up! shut up! I can't take it any more! (*He comes up behind the* WOMAN *and putting his scarf round her neck tries to strangle her.*)

WOMAN: What the hell are you doing? Are you out of your mind? Bastard! Coming to my house to make me commit suicide.

MAN: It's your own fault. You keep on provoking me. Don't you see – I felt like killing you.

WOMAN: It did cross my mind. But calm down. Look at your stomach – it's swelling. If you're ashamed to go into the bathroom just get rid of it here. It's only hot air after all. Anyway I'm just like your mother. I'll put on a nice record, then you can relax.

MAN: Stop it! You're a bitch.

WOMAN: So I'm a bitch! I try to laugh things off – to cool it so that you don't feel guilty. OK – do you want to hear the truth? I am dying with fright. You should have seen the eyes you made. You looked like the Pope when people talk about contraceptives.

MAN: Sure – I can imagine. But I felt so got at. The idea that you wanted to leave me for good. I felt so desperate. Antonia – I love you. (*He tries to embrace her.*)

WOMAN: Stop! I'm suffocating.

MAN: Take your clothes off – please. Give me a kiss.

WOMAN: Yes, I'll give you a kiss – but wait a minute. You're splitting my dress – and breaking my ribs.

MAN: Let's make love. (*He takes off her skirt and boots.*)

WOMAN: Here? Now? But I was going out, darling. I have a date.

MAN: Yes – now – this minute. Let's make love. I'll help you to get your clothes off. (*He makes her lie on the table.*)

WOMAN: The telephone! (*He takes the telephone out from under her back.*)

MAN: Hello? There's no one there. I need you to prove to me –

WOMAN: Prove what?

MAN: That I still mean something to you. (*He unzips his trousers and begins to take them off.*)

WOMAN: You're right. It's a question of pride for you. Yes, I love you. I've been longing for this moment. I love you . . . You're the only one. You're the greatest bastard on earth!

MAN: You really have gone out of your mind!

WOMAN: Just look at yourself. With your pants – you're a sight! Who do you think you are?

MAN: But I love you. After all what have I done? I only wanted to make love to you.

WOMAN: So that's all he wanted! For years now you didn't even know I existed. You didn't even see me. And now that there's this atomic scientist . . . the atomic peril – we have to make love right away on the small table. With the telephone sticking into my back! And then he talks about an open couple! No – all you want is to get possession of what is yours by law. You can lend me out if the conditions are spelled-out clearly but never let go of me. If you could you'd brand me on the bottom with a red-hot iron – like a cow.

MAN: Now you're exaggerating – on the wrist would do. You're talking like one of those old-hat feminists. What are you doing – getting dressed? So you really don't want to?

But that means it's really finished. Curtains! May I know what's got into you?

WOMAN: Who knows what's got into me.

MAN: You seem to me to have shot off at a tangent. You seem to have become – I don't know what to call it – I know! – a complete stranger – something from another world. I love you just as much as before. Try to come to yourself again. The person who insults me – who swears at me – who tries to throw herself out of the window – who shoots at me and misses. That's the Antonia I like best. Come to yourself.

WOMAN: Come to myself? Poor desperate Antonia? Throw yourself out of the window on Thursday – hang yourself on Friday – rest on Sunday. Find your ego. How banal you are! All that stupid rational crap! 'No I can't come out today – I'm looking for my real self.' My ego. Who's got at my ego? It was here – next to the telephone. I can't find it any more. Who's taken it? Excuse, but didn't you see my real self going past? Yes – my real self – it was on a bicycle with its oedipus complex on the crossbar.

MAN: Listen to her – just listen. What irony – what language – what a vocabulary! And then she gets pissed off if I say she's learned it all from that professor. Do you mind telling me one thing – how did you get to know him?

WOMAN: Through his daughter.

MAN: So the Brain has a daughter.

WOMAN: Yes – she's fifteen. I knew her already from the committee on drug addicts.

MAN: You mean one of the girls that works along with you.

WOMAN: No, she's the drug addict.

MAN: She's hooked?

WOMAN: Yes, we're trying to get her off with Methadone. But it's difficult. I got to know her father through her.

MAN: (*with ill-concealed pleasure*) The professor has a fifteen-year-old daughter who takes drugs?

WOMAN: Did you hear how you said that?

MAN: How?

WOMAN: Look – I know you. You almost sounded pleased.

MAN: What at?

WOMAN: At finding out the professor has a drug addict for a daughter.

MAN: You're mad – as if I –

WOMAN: Look me in the eyes!

MAN: OK then – it's true. Spit in my face if you like – you're right – I am a worm. This prof. was beginning to get on my tits – too good to be true – young, witty, bang up-to-date with everything – everything about him the tops. Oh but at last he's fallen down over something.

WOMAN: No, it's you that has fallen down. Do you know what you are?

MAN: Don't tell me. I know it all. I know that today to manage to bring up a child without its being warped by violence – or getting mixed up with drugs – it's like winning the pools – and just as possible.

WOMAN: Well then?

MAN: I'm disgusted with myself – I have to admit it. But still I was pleased. The rich sweet pleasure of the reactionary!

WOMAN: You should be ashamed of yourself. Who was this I married? If you'd got to know him the way I did! He was an empty shell, grey – he seemed done in.

MAN: Really! I'm beginning to like him.

WOMAN: He was desperate. 'I haven't given this child of mine anything – never – a few hugs, silly things – but real affection – I never even tried. I always thought about myself – only myself – and about my career.'

MAN: And you said to him: 'No – don't say that, professor! It's not your fault – it's society's fault.'

WOMAN: Listen – don't start sending me up.

MAN: Didn't you console him, then?

WOMAN: If anyone needed to be consoled then it was me.

MAN: So you kept each other company?

WOMAN: More or less. Then one day I said: 'Listen – don't let's go on weeping and wringing our hands.' We were talking about missiles – about Molesworth and disarmament and we were saying how little people care. 'What about us,' I said, 'it's not as if we do much!' 'Let's go on the next demo.'

MAN: When was this?

WOMAN: A month ago.

MAN: I'm sorry – but didn't you go to Cheltenham to see that cousin of yours who got herself pregnant and had to have an abortion?

WOMAN: That was the story for the husband.

MAN: OK. Apart from the fact that you really disappoint me – you two intellectual snobs – caught up in protest politics and out to Molesworth along with a bunch of left-over hippies. And a dozen lunatic masochists who want to get beaten up by the police.

WOMAN: You really are reactionary!

MAN: What do you mean reactionary? No one believes in demos like that any more, the real Left keeps clear of them.

WOMAN: What do you mean keeps clear of them! What about the last CND demo in Trafalgar Square?

MAN: Another big cosy get-together – sort of carnival – that's OK in London but who's going to go to Molesworth? A couple of MPs from the Labour Left – some Euro communists and a load of feminists.

WOMAN: That's just what we thought. 'Let's go along anyway.'

MAN: So how did you go?

WOMAN: Motorbike.

MAN: You must have been keen!

WOMAN: Why keen? Motorcycling's a hobby like any other.

MAN: Maybe I can see you – with all the gear – boots, leather jacket, helmet on a roaring Suzuki.

WOMAN: You're wrong. It was a Guzzi.

MAN: So he's mad about Italy. With you huddled up at the back. Go on, tell me the rest.

WOMAN: We stopped off at Lincoln.

MAN: Lincoln! That was a bit out of your way.

WOMAN: We sort of didn't feel like the demo any more. It's not as if the danger of atomic war has really got to the masses. And Lincoln is lovely. Remember we went there once.

MAN: I remember.

WOMAN: This was different. So lovely. We walked about. Looked at the cathedral. Had a meal at that restaurant – it's in the Good Food Guide –

MAN: Board and lodging. But even then you didn't manage to make love.

WOMAN: Why? How do you know?

MAN: You told me a while ago. How you felt inhibited.

WOMAN: But only as far as York.

MAN: A tour of the cathedral towns! So you lost your inhibitions in York.

WOMAN: It was marvellous. In a bed and breakfast. The professor wanted to buy the bed – but the landlady wouldn't sell it. Good heavens – what's the time? It's more than half an hour since he called. Damn it – it's your fault, making me chatter on like an idiot. Come on – on your way. No, not that way – go out by the back door. I don't want you to risk meeting him on the stairs.

MAN: So you're going to throw me out by the back door. I used to be your husband – now I'm the milkman.

WOMAN: All right – if you're so easily hurt go out any way you like but put a move on!

MAN: No.

WOMAN: What do you mean No?

MAN: I'm not moving from here. I've had second thoughts. I'm going to wait for him. I want to see him face to face.

WOMAN: Please – don't spoil everything. Get out.

MAN: No!

WOMAN: Are you out of your mind? You promised.

MAN: I didn't promise any damn thing. It is my inalienable right to meet the lover of my wife. I want to look him in the eyes and if, when he looks at me, he so much as moves a muscle of his face – contemptuous like – and does the rock-musician bit I'll smash his guitar over his head.

WOMAN: You're a bastard. I mean to say – first you do everything to make me go along with this disgusting idea of the open couple – so as to be modern and civilised. It makes me want to throw up but – I go along with it to make you happy. I feel bad about it but you go on and on at me and I get round to the idea of looking for a man. I find one. I like him. I fall in love and now, you bastard, you have to wreck everything for me and let him see you as you are – a miserable disgusting creep. And then you want to break his electric guitar as well. Why don't you say you wish I was dead. All right – you know what? This time I'll really do it. The gas – I'll turn on the gas. (*She runs to the kitchen.*)

MAN: (*stopping her*) Stop! Don't waste gas. I'm going – but by the window so you won't have to go through with having to introduce me – if that's what's worrying you. But this time it's for good! (*He climbs onto the window-sill.*)

WOMAN: Don't be an idiot! Get down from there. You're simply ridiculous.

MAN: What do you mean – when you get up on the window-sill it's tragic – it's high drama. I get up and it's ridiculous and embarrassing.

WOMAN: That's right – it's a question of style. Come on – get down!

MAN: What else can I do? If you don't play along there's no drama in it. I always gave you a hand – caught you by the ankle – begged you –

WOMAN: But how am I holding you back – how? Because if you jump you're so overweight you'll take me with you. And just now I don't want to die for real. Come on – get down. Think of your funeral. It'd be like a demo. All your women behind the hearse. Think how unpleasant it would be – all pushing and shoving to show how cut up they were. A couple jump into the grave – the one with the ice-cream weeping all over the coffin.

MAN: OK, go on taking the piss! (*He gets down from the window.*) All right – now you'll see (*He seizes the gun.*) when you made your scene it was almost empty – but this time I've put the bullets in – now it's loaded. (*He fills the magazine.*)

WOMAN: But why waste them all? One will do. Give over – was I as silly-looking as that? Hand it over – don't be a lunatic. You really might let one off. (*Tries to get the gun from him.*)

MAN: Let go – I'm going to shoot myself. (*A shot goes off.*)

WOMAN: Idiot. You fired.

MAN: OK – no harm done. It missed.

WOMAN: What do you mean missed? It hit me right in the foot.

MAN: Oh I'm sorry. (*Passes her the crutch.*)

WOMAN: The great thing about this house is that everything's laid on. There's always a crutch handy. You're a disaster. You're useless. You can't even commit suicide without dragging your wife into it.

MAN: You're right. I'm a washout.

WOMAN: Listen, washout. Since I'm bleeding and, apart from anything else making a mess of the carpet, would you mind going to the bathroom and getting me a towel – a bandage – anything.

MAN: Sure – right away. Just as well – can only be a graze. (*He goes to the bathroom. There's a sound of running water. He comes back with a towel, a bandage, disinfectant etc.*)

WOMAN: Yes, it's just a scratch – just like in a film – the heroine is never badly wounded – otherwise – I'm pleased because the treatment for this sort of wound is very slimming! Did I hear you turn on the bath?

MAN: Yes, I did.

WOMAN: Why? If you feel like having a bath then go home.

MAN: At home I don't have a bath and the shower doesn't work.

WOMAN: What doesn't work? That's enough – I've had it. Get out. Can't you understand I don't want him to find you here?

MAN: But I won't be in the way – you see. When the Brain of Britain arrives he can help you to pull me out of the bath.

WOMAN: Look – I've got other things to do with the Brain of Britain – as you call him – in any case why should the two of us pull you out of the bath?

MAN: Because you wouldn't manage alone. Corpses are heavy.

WOMAN: That's great – my husband drowns himself in my bath. With my plastic flowered cap on his head to stop getting his hair wet! Listen – to drown in my bath you need a superhuman effort. Just think – to lie down under the water with your nose plugged and suffocate yourself – that takes guts. You wouldn't manage, being you!

MAN: Don't worry. I've had another idea. Once I'm in the bath with the hair-dryer in my hand all I have to do is to press that button there and Boom! There's a tremendous flash and that's that. Electrocuted.

WOMAN: So you saw Goldfinger the other evening on Channel Four.

MAN: I don't need a film or a professor of physics to give me ideas – I get them on my own!

WOMAN: Shitty ideas!

MAN: All right. Excuse me a minute, I have to get ready. (*He goes into the bathroom.*) I have to undress.

WOMAN: You're going to commit suicide in the nude.

MAN: Certainly – I have a certain style. I don't suppose you want me to get into the bath with jacket and trousers on . . . (*He shuts the bathroom door.*)

WOMAN: (*knocking on the door*) Stop playing the silly ass and come out of there. All right – maybe I did make mistakes, I went a bit far humiliating you like that. Come out. Talk it over. Let's discuss things like civilised people. Come out. (*She squints through the keyhole.*)

MAN: It's too late, love. And don't peep. Aren't you ashamed?

WOMAN: He's mad. He really has plugged in the hair-dryer. Stop!

MAN: Sure. That way you'll learn not to humiliate me. I want to die. God, the water's cold. Doesn't the boiler work in this house?

WOMAN: Stop. It's not true – any of it. I made it all up. The professor doesn't exist.

MAN: (*puts his head round the door*) So you made up the Brain of Britain. And when the telephone rang a little while ago you did it all by ventriloquism, is that it? (*He comes in wrapped up more or less in a towel. He has the dryer in his hand and points it at his wife.*)

WOMAN: But there was someone on the line – only they had got the wrong number and rang off. I went on pretending it was him.

MAN: My compliments on your acting. But it doesn't hold water. You're trying to distract me and make me lose time – so the professor will arrive shortly and the two of you will jump on me and stop me. (*He backs away pointing the dryer like a gun.*) Stop. Don't come any closer or I'll jump.

WOMAN: For goodness' sakes don't do it with a hair-dryer. I know – let's call the Atomic Energy Commission. I'm going to ring Enquiries and get the number. (*She does so.*) I'll have a good laugh when you say: 'Excuse me but have you a head of department who writes rock numbers?' (*On the phone.*) Hello – can you give me the number of the Atomic Energy Commission? (*The MAN cuts off the phone.*) Aren't you going to speak?

MAN: So I fell for it like an idiot. You really did invent the lot.

WOMAN: Phew – the fright you gave me. Are you feeling a bit calmer now? Relax. It would have been such a tragedy! OK, I made it all up but I did it to make you see how much a person suffers. Yes, you fell for it but –

MAN: No – you fell for it.

WOMAN: How?

MAN: All that stuff about suicide!

WOMAN: So it was all –

MAN: Look at it – it's burnt out. I just did it to make a scene. I'd no intention of taking a risk and ending up flambé – like some sort of zombie. Darling, I see daylight ahead!

WOMAN: You made it all up?

MAN: Yes – it was a joke. (*Laughs.*) Anyway I should say thank you – it was a gas. How does that song go? 'You came up on the telephone . . .'

WOMAN: You're a despicable bastard.

MAN: Stop it, Urania. (*The bell rings.*)

MAN: You go. I'm enjoying myself. (*He goes on singing and sending the song up.*) 'And you appeared on my screen you blew my circuits.' (*The* WOMAN *goes to the door. There's a man in his forties. It's the* PROFESSOR.)

PROFESSOR: Sorry I'm a little late. (*He kisses her.*)

MAN: Who's he?

PROFESSOR: Is this your husband? Am I wrong or was he humming my song?

MAN: Who is he, please?

WOMAN: But, love, who should it be – the rock professor.

MAN: Him. No. The Brain exists. He really does exist! (*He grabs the dryer and rushes into the bathroom. There is an explosion and a huge flash.*)

WOMAN: Oh no!

An Ordinary Day

translated by JOE FARRELL

An Ordinary Day was first performed at the Teatro Nuovo, Milan, on 9 October 1986.

An Ordinary Day was first performed in this translation, by Borderline Theatre Company, who toured the play in May/June 1988 with the following cast:

JULIA	Juliet Cadzow
TOM	Bill McElhaney
JIMMY	Laurie Ventry
FEMALE CALLERS	Barbara Rafferty Elizabeth Philips Scot
POLICEMAN	Lawrie McNichol

Directed by Morag Fullerton

*A one room studio-flat, with cooker and bed-settee.
Photographer's lamps with spotlight and reflector.*

*A woman is fiddling about with a video-cassette recorder. She
checks the monitor and big screen situated at the far edge of the
stage to ensure that they are in working order. She moves,
poses, observes herself but is plainly unhappy with the result.
She claps her hands and immediately one of the arc lights goes
on. She shifts the reflector. She changes her dress. She inserts a
shade and a coloured gel into one of the lamps. Now she is
apparently more or less satisfied.*

JULIA: Perhaps I am too far back . . . it's too big that way . . .
just look at the bags under those eyes. I'll need to open out
the light. (*She claps her hands again and the light attached to
the reflector goes on.*) Let's try the automatic follow-shot.
(*She switches it on.*) Come on – over here. (*She moves left
and right, followed by the camera on a tripod on wheels.*)
Good boy! The only thing that follows me now is the tripod.
(*The phone rings.*) No, I've no time. The answering
machine's turned on, so just you talk to it quietly and don't
bother me. (*She goes over to a coat-hanger where an
enormous assortment of clothes are hanging.*) How about
this little number? An ankle-length dress. (*She puts it on,
stands in front of the camera and has a look at herself in the
monitor.*) Good God! See how overweight it makes me.
Obese. Maybe I am fat! If I come on like that, he'll take me
for Cyril Smith. I can just see him ordering up two tins of
some fancy sea-weed for slimmers. For a time like this a

wedding gown would be just the thing. Yeah, but with a
spare tyre like mine, I could hardly get a leg in. Anyway,
God knows where the wedding dress ended up. Probably I
made a tent out of it.

*She continues to change the dress at top speed, in a kind of
quick-change routine. It might be helpful if she went behind a
screen where two stage hands could help with the costumes.*

No, this one's better – nice and simple, in tune with what's
going on. No, this might be just the ticket, loose fitting and
serious . . . I've got it, I've got it. A party frock. (*She looks at
herself for a moment.*) All I need is a bunch of bananas on
my head and I'd look like Joan Rivers on an off day. No, no!
– No strong colours – a Social Democratic outfit – (*Putting
on a dress picked at random.*) – afternoon tea in foggy
London town. Here we are . . . all systems go . . . (*She
presses a button on the video-cassette recorder.*) Action!
(*She runs and places herself in front of the camera. A
moment of confusion and embarrassed silence.*) Bloody
hell! With all these things I was just bursting to say . . . now
look at me, struck dumb . . . Ah yes, the hands – let's kick
off with the hands. (*She runs over, turns back the tape, and
starts again.*) Action! (*She takes a deep breath and holds her
hands out towards the camera.*)

Look at my hands . . . go on, have a good look . . . do you see
them? They are right in front of your nose . . . do you
recognise them? Big . . . fleshy . . . do you recognise them?
You have held them in yours . . . you have kissed them. And
the thing behind them is my face . . . do you recognise me?
It's me, I'm your wife! (*She stops. She goes over and runs
back the tape.*)

I must be out of my mind. What way is that to begin? It
sounds like a horror film . . . Zombies On The Prowl. I
don't want to scare him stiff with those two monstrous
hands. And what made me say 'Right in front of your nose'?
Who's he supposed to be anyway? Pinocchio? In front of
your very eyes sounds better. And then that 'It's me, your
wife.' It comes over like the voice of God. (*Shouts.*) It's me,

me, your wife . . . come back from the dead to throttle you.
Poor thing.

No, that's not going to do. We need a new opening,
something completely different. (*Switches on the tape
recorder which produces a love song*.) What made me
launch with the hands? Maybe I should draw up a plan of
what I'm going to say. Got it. I know how to get going: with
the letter. (*Sets up the video, gets her pose right. Silence for a
few minutes, then, with the music still playing in the
background*.)

Hi! It's me, Julia, I've just got to talk to you. Are you sitting
comfortably? Then I'll begin. I know . . . for one thing this is
not the ordinary way of communicating. I wrote you a letter
. . . but I didn't post it. I'd rather read it to you. Anyway, I'd
rather you were able to watch me when I'm talking to you.
You see, the fact that afterwards . . . I mean, right now for
you . . . the fact that you will be there watching me . . . it
gives me encouragement . . . gives me strength . . . and I
really need that. When you receive this video-letter. (*The
soft music ends. A piece of rock music explodes from the
tape-recorder*.)

My God, what a fright! Just a minute till I turn this thing
down . . . (*Adjusts the sound*.) I'm sorry, but rock music
brings me out in spots. As I was saying. Thanks to the
mediation of this electronic instrument . . . (*The phone
rings*.) Dear God, not now. I should have pulled out the
plug. Oh how stupid I am. I have put on the ansaphone. I
bet you do not remember what day it is tomorrow. It is our
anniversary. It's exactly one year since we separated.
During this year, I thought about you a lot . . . then less and
less . . . and now . . . I hardly think about you at all. I still
have some feelings for you. To me, you are like a relative
. . . an older cousin . . . one of the family, a nice sort,
somebody that you like to see every so often . . . at funerals,
weddings, christenings . . . So it seems quite natural to turn
to you for . . . (*She is suddenly interrupted*.) Excuse me.
Somebody's on the phone. I can't make out who. I've lost

my concentration. I'll go and unplug the machine, then we'll get started again.

She switches off the video-recorder, switches off the arc lights with a clap of her hands and moves to the telephone answering machine. She presses a button and listens.

JEAN'S VOICE: Hello. Forgive me for disturbing you at this hour, doctor. This is Jean Alred, do you remember me? I am the one with the burn on the buttocks because of the brick. I have to talk to you – no, not because of my buttocks. Oh, Doctor, I'm very low. I hope I'll be able to contact you in a couple of hours. If you do go out, would you leave a message on your answering machine, so that I'll be able to trace you. I'm desperate. I'll phone back.

JULIA: (*puzzled*) Doctor? She's got a burn on the buttocks and she's feeling down. She must have got my number mixed up with some analyst. Funny analyst all the same, who goes around burning her clients' bums.

She claps her hands and the lights which she has dimmed come back up. She puts the video-recorder back on and goes round in front of the camera.

Sorry about that, but a funny thing has just happened. Someone got the wrong number and took me for a psychiatrist. She was looking for help . . . from me! She has stumbled onto the right woman and no mistake. A right nutcase. Yes, that's not just a manner of speaking. I am quite, completely crazy, mad, ready for the strait-jacket . . . but lucid. You have no idea how many times, at the dead of night, I got up, intending to come round to your place and do you in. I mean it! I even bought a gun. That's right, with a proper gun user's licence. Once I even thought of shadowing you while you were going to the station to pick up your new woman, and then just as the train was drawing in, I was going to give you a little push under the wheels. Scared? Well, relax, take it easy. Have a drop of whisky and wipe your brows with an ice cube. All this happened at the very beginning, when my metabolism was altering, for my metabolism was totally, one hundred per cent

dependent on you. And I thought I was a liberated woman!
I have really made an effort, you know. I have even done
some dreadful exercises. Look at this. You see what I mean.
You have to get yourself into a position like this. Come on.
Have a go. Don't get embarrassed, now. You have to raise
one leg, slowly, very, very slowly, until you reach knee
level, and then you swing one across the other. Gently does
it. Much more gently. It should take you about two hours to
get it up, two hours to let it back down, that's four hours a
leg, eight hours all in all. And so the day goes by. Then you
go to bed and after all that . . . you still can't get a wink of
sleep!

That's the idea. On you go. It'll do you the world of good.

I've been through one hell of a time. But here I am, I've
made it. Or maybe I am just kidding myself that I have
made it. Paranoia? Could be. But I am not well. The
problem is that I have no interests. I do not give a damn
about anyone. Not even about my job . . . advertising! Hour
after hour, racking my brains to think up some way to make
people buy things they could do perfectly well without. It's
hell with other people, it's hell on my own. For some time
I've been wondering what I'm doing here in this world. If
you want a laugh, I could recite 'To be or not to be that is the
question'. Don't worry. It was a joke.

Nevertheless, I would like to talk to you about my
existential problem. Do you know, I have discovered that
living in this world is all a question of keeping up with the
play . . . adapting and accepting the ritual . . . if you don't,
you just throw in your hand. You know, like, when you're
playing poker and you get one of those dud hands and there
is no way you can do anything with it. So what do you do?
You just throw it in. You sit it out. Well then, here's me,
with a hand that would make you vomit . . . but it's not a
matter of bad luck. I've been cheated. Yes, yes, I know, I
could shrug my shoulders . . . wait for a good hand . . . then I
could do the cheating. It is just that . . . that kind of game
doesn't interest me any more. Everything is so savage,
barbaric, improbable or downright vulgar. It's all over in

about twenty minutes, just like those soap operas on the TV.

I know what you are going to say. 'Well, what do you expect? We are living in a TV culture. You've got to make the best of it, put up with it . . . don't aim too high, be like the rest.' I had worked out a programme for myself, with stacks of wonderful ideas, padded out with dreams . . . and, with beautiful Utopias into the bargain. And why not? I threw myself into it, and I found myself flying headfirst into a swimming pool, a moment after they had drained out all the water.

I could hear them guffawing all around me. 'Get a load of this one. She still believes in fairy tales, in togetherness, in changing the world. You'll need to be a bit more down to earth, a bit more realistic, Julia.' It makes me sick, this 'realistic'. No, no, I am not going to comply. Arse-lickers, opportunists, hypocrites, people who would trample over other people's faces . . . you see them hawking their own self-respect, offering you their bums. No, I don't want to put up with it . . . I won't comply . . . I'll throw in my hand . . . I'll sit this one out. What is it they call it, the dead hand, the dummy hand? What difference does it make? What's all the fuss? What is this death, anyway? It is merely the moment the machine stops churning . . . breaks down . . . is ready to be thrown out . . . and so somebody comes and tosses it on the heap. In my case the whole central system has seized up. Yes, I still move, talk, even tell jokes, but it's a trick. It's really just the inertia force. I'm a cog that is worn out, waiting to be thrown away. I've got to give the final touch, switch off the power. No, don't you get agitated. In any case, when you get the video-tape, it will be all over.

(*Phone rings*.) Damnation, the phone at a time like this! I'm sorry, but this time I've switched off the answering machine. I'll have to answer. (*Goes to the phone*.) Hello?

JEAN'S VOICE: Good evening, Doctor, at last I've got you.

JULIA: Again? Wait a minute till I turn off the camera and put out the lights. (*Goes to switch them off*.)

JEAN'S VOICE: What were you saying?

JULIA: I was saying that you've got the wrong number.

JEAN'S VOICE: What do you mean? What number is that? Just a minute, is that not 611 3002?

JULIA: Yes, certainly.

JEAN'S VOICE: Then it's the right number.

JULIA: It might be the right number, but it's not the right person, at least not the person you're looking for. Excuse me, where did you get this number?

JEAN'S VOICE: In the magazine . . . there, what's it called, wait a minute . . . here it is, it's called *Health*, and on page 38 there's an article all about you.

JULIA: Who? You?

JEAN'S VOICE: You, you! It says 'Famous Analyst Completes Specialist Research in Japan.'

JULIA: I've never been to Japan.

JEAN'S VOICE: Ah no. Well, you know how it is, you can never trust what you read in the papers, but the important thing is that the method is the right one and that it works, don't you agree?

JULIA: What method?

JEAN'S VOICE: Yours. The one that is described here: The psycho-respiratory technique with the emission of appropriate vocalisations.

JULIA: And what happens . . .

JEAN'S VOICE: You attain diapason. Diapason employed by the holy men of Indonesia who thus manage to levitate. Isn't that right, Doctor, that they manage to rise?

JULIA: But, I don't know . . . but why, instead of rising . . . do you really want to rise . . . what are you, some kind of home-made bread?

JEAN'S VOICE: No, I don't want to rise at all. The very idea! My husband can't stand me when I'm just normal, standing on the floor. I'd hate to think what he'd do if I went floating around the house, banging my head against the ceiling.

He'd be only too glad to get his gun and bring me down with a bang! All I want is to get rid of this neurosis of mine, just like you say in your article.

JULIA: What did you say this magazine was called? *Health*. I get it sent to me. (*Goes to search in a paper rack.*) If it's the last issue . . . just a minute, I must have put it . . . here we are, page 38 you say.

JEAN'S VOICE: Yes, if you look at the bottom of the page, you'll see the phone number as well.

JULIA: You're quite right, they've got my number here. What kind of joke is this? Obviously there's been a mistake.

JEAN'S VOICE: No doubt, a private number. They've got no sense of manners, you just don't go handing out a private number. It's been a bit of good luck for me, because I can ask your advice personally. What do you think I should do, Doctor? I might be pregnant. I'm waiting to check the blue window.

JULIA: Now look here, I've already told you. I am not the doctor you are looking for.

JEAN'S VOICE: I can quite believe it. You are not an obstetrician, you're an analyst. The only thing that interests me is to know whether these exercises with the brick would be ill-advised in the event of the tests telling me . . . 'Yes, you are pregnant.'

JULIA: Look, please, quite apart from the fact that you have caught me at a somewhat, shall we say, delicate moment, listen to me, whatever the blue window says, I cannot give you any advice, because I have no medical qualifications.

JEAN'S VOICE: Ah, you're one of these fly-by-night people! Doesn't matter to me, though, I had all my teeth done by a very fine dental mechanic, and he was one of those cowboy operators. It cost me half of what I would have paid on the NHS, though.

JULIA: I'm not a dentist either. I work in advertising.

JEAN'S VOICE: Medical advertising?

JULIA: No, travel and holiday advertising, films, videos, that sort of thing.

JEAN'S VOICE: So what are you doing in the house of a medical analyst? Are you a relative?

JULIA: What do you mean relative? This is my house!

JEAN'S VOICE: I get it, the analyst is staying with you. Let me speak to her, if you don't mind.

JULIA: (*exasperated*) No, I won't let you speak to her. I cannot let you speak to her!

JEAN'S VOICE: That's lovely that is! And why not?

JULIA: Because she's not here . . . she's away checking for blue windows.

JEAN'S VOICE: For blue windows?

JULIA: (*as though insane*) That's right, for blue windows. Then she gives them to hysterical women who find relief from tension by getting pregnant.

JEAN'S VOICE: (*puzzled*) Pregnant?

JULIA: Yes with a cowboy or a dental mechanic, a fly-by-night operator . . . Is that clear?

JEAN'S VOICE: (*terrified*) No, but I think I've got the wrong number, I'm sorry. (*She hangs up.* JULIA *does the same.*)

JULIA: At long bloody last. It would drive you nuts, all this. God help any analyst who ends up having to treat her! (*Picks up the magazine and reads it.*) There's one born every day . . . do people really believe this garbage? (*Reads aloud.*) 'Stretch yourself full length on a table, placing a brick beneath your buttocks, move your knees apart while keeping your heels closely together. Let your head hang over the edge of the table. Take deep breaths and hum the sounds A-u-o-i-e-u-o, on the Do-Ray notes until you reach Fa. Then come back to Do.'

Did you ever hear the like? (*She sings out the notes making the whole thing ridiculous.*) AU OO EU OOO, IAUU! There are people who actually believe this! Some folk have done time for less . . . they should put this one up against a wall! (*She tries again.*) AU OH OOO UIOAA. (*Switches

on the video-recorder, goes back in front of the camera. The
lights go up again.)

Here I am again. I was saying that I have decided to end it
all. You'll be asking yourself why I'm telling you all this.
Perhaps you don't believe what I was saying a few moments
ago. Maybe you think I'm out for revenge because you were
so keen to reduce me to despair, or maybe you imagine that
I'm trying to make you shoulder the blame for this insane
act I'm going to commit. It's not that. You can put your
mind at rest. This last little chat has as its overriding
objective . . . is that not good, eh? Quite a turn of phrase. . . .
Has the overriding objective of removing ambiguities,
misunderstandings, and . . . and arrogance. I mean the
greatest arrogance of all, that of believing yourself the cause
of my suicide. I will not grant you that satisfaction. You
would have quite liked that, wouldn't you? I can just see
you, preening yourself. The man whose face is lined with
the tragic memory of the woman who slew herself for love of
him. Who could resist such a man? And when they put up a
monument to your wild love affairs, am I supposed to be the
little female crouched at your feet? Andromeda bleeding to
death before the great Perseus! Not on your life! It has
nothing to do with you! Divest yourself of the laurels of
Perseus. (*Interrupting herself.*) Perseus! What the hell has
Perseus got to do with it? (*She claps her hands, the lights go
down, she switches off the camera and turns on the video-
recorder. The picture of* JULIA, *playing the part just
recorded, appears on the screen*).

The first bit is OK, then I started to waffle. (*Goes and lies
down.*) Take it easy . . . let's just calm down . . . I mean, it is
not as though it is one of the commercial breaks that you
dream up on the spur of the moment. This is the last break
of my life, so it had better be good. This is one for the
archives. I can just see the whole family gathering for the
festive season, Christmas, New Year . . . all sitting round
the table and somebody saying: 'Let's have a look at Julia's
video . . . let's listen to what she said before she did herself
in. It's always good for a laugh.'

Calm down . . . there's still plenty of time before night . . .
you've got it in you . . . first I'll make myself something to
eat . . . the last supper! All by myself; not even Judas to keep
me company. I never thought I'd have been able to do all
this with such detachment. Is this the catharsis of the return
to the warm womb, as Seneca put it, while he was slashing
his wrists, in the bath? In fact God knows how many times
I've read about people hanging themselves, shooting
themselves or slashing their wrists and all the time nobody
had the slightest idea that they were getting ready for the
great deed. All calm, all normal, as if it were an ordinary
day. That's just how I intend going about it. An ordinary
day. I'll even stick to my diet today. So, today is Thursday,
what's on the menu today? (*Looks up a kind of list.*)
Chicken, boiled chicken, a whole chicken is permissible!
An orgy! Carrot juice. These jockeys' diets are just the job.

*Switches on the television, where a soap opera is being
shown.* JULIA *takes the chicken from the fridge and places it
on the table with evident disgust. While watching the pictures
from the soap opera,* JULIA *cleans the vegetables and puts
them into the pot along with the chicken. Once she has
completed this operation, she sets the table with meticulous
care. At the tear jerking climax of the programme, she goes
and flops onto a settee.*

MALE (*on TV*): Cast your eye on this photo. What does it tell
you?

FEMALE (*on TV*): It's him, my husband! But who is that little
whore with her arm around his waist?

MALE: That's no little whore. That's the daughter of his best
friend and business associate.

FEMALE: Who? Tom?

MALE: Yes, him. You can bet that if Tom finds out that his
daughter is rolling about on his best friend's bed every
afternoon, he'll tear him apart, limb from limb.

FEMALE: Where did you get this photograph?

MALE: Someone from the Argo Agency took it.

FEMALE: A private investigation agency? You mean you set one of these infamous dicks on the heels of my husband?

MALE: No, I set the private dick on the heels of her, Elsa, Tom's daughter. No one was more amazed than me to find your husband mixed up in this business.

FEMALE: You see what a bastard he is! But what gave you the idea of shadowing that Elsa in the first place?

MALE: I told you that before you and I fell in love, I had an affair with a girl . . . well, that girl was her, Elsa. But later I began to harbour the suspicion that, although she was still seeing me, she was two-timing me with someone else, and that someone else was none other than your husband.

FEMALE: Antony, you rat! However, I'm glad it was him who lured that simpering little bitch away from you.

MALE: Excellent. Then you'll be happy to know that his affair with Elsa is only a cover-up.

FEMALE: A cover-up for what?

MALE: The investigator also shadowed your husband's business associate, and stumbled on the fact that Tom and your Antony are lovers.

FEMALE: Oh no . . . I'll kill myself. (*Bursts out laughing.*) Ha, ha! What did you expect? Did you really think I was going to kill myself? Ha! Ha! Well, I'm sorry to disappoint you. I knew all along! Ha! Ha!

MALE: Then I hope you'll be able to laugh as heartily at this. Tom's got AIDS.

FEMALE: No, that's a lie. It's all an invention.

MALE: Yes, and was it an invention to have him observed in the very hospital where they were carrying out the tests? But it was worthwhile, because in that way I found out that your husband has got AIDS too.

FEMALE: I knew this all along as well. It was me that passed it on to him.

MALE: What?

FEMALE: Yes, my dear, I've got AIDS – so I have passed it on to you too.

MALE: How can you be sure? Perhaps I didn't catch it.

FEMALE: Just go and have a little look in the mirror. You've got so many spots all over your skin that you look like a giraffe without the neck.

MALE: It's true. I hoped against hope that it was only leprosy. How is it that there are no marks on you?

FEMALE: I am a healthy carrier of the disease.

MALE: What about Tom and Antony?

FEMALE: They are clean carriers as well. You, dear John, are the only one who has gone bad. Goodbye, John!

MALE: But I love you. Don't leave me! Don't leave me! I love you.

FEMALE: I love you too, John . . . but I'm not leaving you. You are leaving us all.

MALE: What do you mean I'm leaving you all?

FEMALE: You see, you're leaving me, you're leaving the world. You are dying, John. Farewell, forever.

JULIA *switches off the TV. Switches on the record player and light, sentimental music fills the room. She absent-mindedly reaches for a bottle on the drinks trolley; immediately a siren begins to screech and a light on top of the fridge – of the same kind as seen on police cars – starts flashing. A loud deep voice rings out.*

VOICE: It is established by sociological research that the social vacuum in the life of the average housewife often leads to alcoholism.

JULIA *angrily replaces the glass and the bottle. Once she does so, the flashing stops and the voice falls silent.*

JULIA: For God's sake, I haven't touched a drop. Alcohol is bad for the liver, the liver swells up, you catch hepatic cirrhosis, your belly gets bloated, bloated, till one day BANG! it blows up and the neighbours phone the council.

Switches on the TV again, to find pictures of a policeman, shots, car chases, explosions. The phone rings and JULIA *automatically picks up the receiver. At the same moment the* POLICEMAN *on the TV screen picks up the receiver of his own phone.* JULIA *does not notice the confusion.*

Hello, who's speaking, please?

POLICEMAN (*on TV*): Yes, madam, what can I do for you?

JULIA: I beg your pardon, it was you who called.

POLICEMAN: Take it easy, don't get excited.

JULIA: I'm perfectly calm, thank you very much. Well then, what are you after?

POLICEMAN: When did all this take place? Let's have a bit of order around here.

JULIA: Whose order, may I ask? It's all perfectly clear. Are you all mad today?

POLICEMAN: Now look here. If you imagine for one minute that the entire city police force is waiting here for the first streetwalker to phone us with a load of old cock . . . I'll come right round and knock some sense into you.

JULIA: How dare . . . (*Realises what has been happening.*) Away and chase yourself. (*Hangs up.*)

POLICEMAN: Hello! Hello! She's hung up, the lousy whore.

JULIA *once again stretches out on the settee. Quite mechanically, she lifts the lid of a cigarette case and picks out a cigarette. She lifts a heavy lighter from the table, and as she does so the pictures on the wall open out to reveal a series of posters with anti-smoking slogans. There is one with the picture of a smoker with a sickly green face, strangled by an enormous cigarette. Another shows a skeleton puffing away with evident delight, while underneath there are legends like . . . 'Your bronchial passages are putrid sponges, sodden with black tar', or 'nicotine equals cancer', or 'smoking ruins your sex life, slows your reflexes and dulls the brain'.*

JULIA: Bloody hell! I set up all those little traps by myself and then I go and forget all about them. No way is it going to be allowed. I am determined to die the very picture of health. No smoking!

She stubs out the cigarette she had just lit in the ash-tray, puts the lighter back on the table and everything goes back to its previous position. Meantime on the television screen, violence, punch-ups, tough interrogations follow one another in quick succession. The telephone rings once again. JULIA makes the mechanical gesture of reaching out for the receiver but stops herself in time.

Eh no, not this time. I'm not falling for it again. (*The telephone continues to ring.*)

POLICEMAN: Would someone out there be good enough to pick up the phone. (*Pointing his finger directly at JULIA.*) Hey, you! Wakey, wakey! I'm talking to you.

JULIA: (*amazed*) Oh, is it my phone? Oh, I am sorry. (*Lifts the receiver.*) Hello!

WOMAN'S VOICE: Good evening, Doctor. How are you? Forgive me if . . .

JULIA: Here we go again. Back to this 'Good evening, Doctor', business.

WOMAN'S VOICE: Did you get my message on your answering machine?

JULIA: Yeah, I got it all right, but I have to say that you are . . .

WOMAN'S VOICE: I know, you're right, Doctor, and I swear that I tried it out but the only result was that, once I lay down on that hot brick, I burned my bum.

JULIA: Listen, will you stop going on about that hot brick and pay attention.

WOMAN'S VOICE: Don't ask me to give up my brick, because, to tell you the truth, madam doctor, the first day it gave me a bit of . . . em . . . pleasure but thereafter . . . the thing is, I have not got a note in my head and I cannot get the harmonies right, especially in the rising scale. Listen . . . A OOUOOAAAUIOUIA . . . AOOUOOAAAUIUOUIAA.

JULIA: (*trying to interrupt*) Oooah. Stop!

WOMAN'S VOICE: You see what I mean about not having a note in my head. So that must be why the treatment is having no effect. Listen, how would it be if instead of trying to make the sounds in a singing voice, I had a go at whistling? I am much better at that. I'll try it out. See what you think. (*Whistles*.)

JULIA: Look, if you don't listen to me, I'm putting the phone down.

WOMAN'S VOICE: All right! Don't get mad, please, I'm listening.

JULIA: It's all a mistake. I am not the analyst you take me for –

WOMAN'S VOICE: But the number . . .

JULIA: The number is the right one . . . but it's also the wrong one, and I am somebody else.

WOMAN'S VOICE: Ah, you're somebody else. So you're another one who's suffering from split personality. (*Laughs*.) Come off it, Doctor . . . I recognise you. That's your voice, the same as before.

JULIA: It's not my fault if the voice is the same. The other one fell into the trap as well.

WOMAN'S VOICE: A trap! Are you having me on, Doctor? I get it. I'm annoying you. I'm annoying you with my problems and so to scare me off, you pretend to be somebody else. You make out you are some hysterical pregnant wife. But it is not going to work, you know. I really am unwell and you are going to have to listen to me.

JULIA: Now that's where you are wrong! This time you have really done it. (*Makes to hang up*.)

WOMAN'S VOICE: Hold it, Doctor. Don't try to hang up on me or I'll come round there and smash up the house.

JULIA: (*to herself*) She can see me!!! (*Into the telephone*.) Now listen here. You don't scare me. Quite apart from the fact that I would really like to know how you would manage to find out where I live, because the magazine only gives the phone number, isn't that so?

WOMAN'S VOICE: Aha! But I phoned up the exchange. I've got a friend who works on the computer section and he gave me the address . . . 138 Bentinck Street, fourth floor, second door on the right, so there.

JULIA: Oh God. Now I'm done for.

WOMAN'S VOICE: Here's me going through this terrible time . . . just you try to give me the shove and I'll be right round there . . . it's only ten minutes you know . . . I'll set fire to your place and I'll shoot you between the eyes. I've got a revolver here, you know. Property of a friend of mine. Understand?

JULIA: I've already told you that you don't frighten me. For your information, I've got a gun as well, so you bring yours round and we can have a shoot-out, like *High Noon* . . . a fight to the death. Anyway, if you get me, so much the better.

WOMAN'S VOICE: I understand. As hard as nails, you are. But I don't mind. Because, my dear doctor, you must admit it is not on to write certain articles in magazines, bringing a glimmer of hope to a poor woman driven to despair by her neurodelirium – and then to create a fuss over a phone call.

JULIA: (*to herself*) Oh God in heaven, is everybody out to get me . . . You can't even kick the bucket in peace. (*Speaking into the phone.*) All right, all right. I'm listening. What can I do for you?

Meantime the action of the detective story continues on the screen. JULIA, *who had been fiddling with the remote control, unintentionally turns up the volume.*

POLICEMAN (*on TV*): Let go of that hysterical bitch . . . can't you see that she's just a schizophrenic whore.

JULIA: (*quickly switching off the TV*) I'm sorry. I didn't mean that.

WOMAN'S VOICE: Did that refer to me? A hysterical bitch! You tell your husband that I . . .

JULIA: No, it wasn't my husband. It was the TV detective.

WOMAN'S VOICE: You mean to tell me there's a TV detective in your house?

JULIA: No, no, I'm not living . . . inside the TV set, if you see what I mean. I just happened to turn up the sound on the . . .

WOMAN'S VOICE: Pull the other one! How did your TV detective know I'm on the game?

JULIA: On the game!

WOMAN'S VOICE: I'm a call-girl, a street-walker, anything you like, Doctor. And don't sound so dumbfounded because I told you all about it the other day in your surgery. You and your husband were the only ones who knew about my schizophrenia. You told me yourself. And tell that bastard of a husband of yours to lay off or I'll blow his brains out as well.

JULIA: Great! So who am I making this video for? Listen here. You keep your hands off my husband. Let him live, so that he dies of despair!

WOMAN'S VOICE: Hello. What have I said? I don't understand.

JULIA: It doesn't matter. Well, hurry up. Tell me what you want.

WOMAN'S VOICE: I don't know. It's just that I've done all the exercises, like you said, but apart from the burns on my bum, nothing has happened. I'm no further forward . . . in fact it's going from bad to worse, because I had a crisis at work . . . bloody awful it was . . . I nearly ended up in the clink for assault.

JULIA: Why? What did you do?

WOMAN'S VOICE: Well, there I was, going about my lawful business, as I was telling you. I was getting him ready.

JULIA: You were getting him ready? Who were you getting ready?

WOMAN'S VOICE: A client. I was practising . . . what do you call it . . . that oral thing that that wanker Reagan in America doesn't like.

JULIA: Ah, I see. Then what happened?

WOMAN'S VOICE: Well, all of a sudden, a fit of rage came over me and I sank my teeth right in.

JULIA: You did what?

WOMAN'S VOICE: Snap . . . just like that. Got the old fangs right round it. Talk about the Hound of the Baskervilles. I didn't let go. He was howling as though it had been chopped off, and he gave me a thump on the head. That wasn't a good idea, because it was like bringing a hammer down on a nutcracker. Snap! You know what I mean. Zak! It jumped right up in the air.

JULIA: His what do you call it!

WOMAN'S VOICE: Just one of his balls. Fortunately it rolled under a cupboard and I managed to pick it up. I put it neatly in a plastic bag with some blocks of ice and rushed at top speed to the nearest casualty ward. You know how in the hospital nowadays they do grafts and things. Anything that falls off they can put back on. It's wonderful.

JULIA: Miracle workers, eh.

WOMAN'S VOICE: I must say he was quite good about it. He didn't even report me. He told the cop on duty that it was a ravenous ape at the zoo who took a swipe at him while he was giving it sweeties. No gratitude, these apes. However, you'll understand that in my line of business I cannot live on with the risk of these crises. Once you have chewed off four or five testicles, the word gets around, and the punters cross the road when they see you coming. So, you tell me, Doctor, what am I going to do?

JULIA: Well, for a start . . . you know those rubber gum shields that boxers put in their mouths to stop their teeth getting knocked out . . . I'd put one over my teeth if I were you . . . and then I'd give the exercises a miss.

WOMAN'S VOICE: Even the humming vowels?

JULIA: Even them. In fact keep your mouth tightly shut, especially when you find it in the vicinity of male genitals, and breathe gently through your nose.

WOMAN'S VOICE: Is that all?

JULIA: There's only one other thing that you should do but it's very important. (*To herself.*) What's going on here?

How did I get myself into this? Here am I playing the agony
auntie. I feel like a life-guard . . . a testicle-guard, more like.
(*Picks up the phone again.*) Now listen carefully.

WOMAN'S VOICE: I promise, I promise.

JULIA: Tomorrow, take the first train and go back home.
You're from Forfar, right?

WOMAN'S VOICE: Not exactly, I'm from Brechin.

JULIA: It's all the same . . . does your mother still live there?

WOMAN'S VOICE: Yes, poor old thing.

JULIA: There you are then. You go back there for a wee
while, at least a month, and you'll see you'll get better. Get
bags of fresh air, do a wee bit of work in the country but
nothing too strenuous. You'll feel a new woman.

WOMAN'S VOICE: Are you sure it works?

JULIA: Couldn't be surer. I've tried it hundreds of times
myself and if you could see me now . . . full of oomph,
up-and-at-'em, you know what I mean? There aren't
enough hours in the day!

WOMAN'S VOICE: God bless you, Doctor. I'll do what you
say. I'll set off right away. You're a saint. I feel better
already. (*She hangs up.* JULIA *does likewise.*)

JULIA: It would drive you mad, this trying to cure madmen
and madwomen. I nearly spoiled everything. If she really
had come round to fight a duel and burn down the house, I'd
have had to postpone the whole thing. And then when
would I have got myself psyched up again to do myself in?
Talk, talk . . . I'm just wasting time . . . I must get my video
done. (*Lights up a cigarette with a worried look.
Immediately, the pictures open out, the siren goes off and the
light begins flashing.*) Oh you're really getting on my nerves.
One cigarette, after all this carry on, that's not too much to
ask. And then, I must concentrate, do you understand?
(JULIA *has the lighter in her hand, and throws it violently
against the wall. A scream is heard.* JULIA *stops in dismay.
The scream comes from the next door flat.*)

FEMALE VOICE (*from next door*): You're a bastard.

JULIA: Oh God! The wall is talking.

FEMALE VOICE: You batter me because I can't defend myself.

JULIA: Ah! The next door neighbours.

MALE VOICE: You're pretty good with your hands yourself – you bastard you.

FEMALE VOICE: You're the bastard. Always at it with that whore of yours.

JULIA: They always quarrel and then they make love.

FEMALE VOICE: I'll kill you. (*A crash, caused by something being thrown, is heard.*)

MALE VOICE: You're mad. You nearly got me on the head . . . put that thing down . . . Jesus Christ, it's bronze.

FEMALE VOICE: I'll break it over your head!

MALE VOICE: I swear to you that there is nothing between me and that woman. Put that thing down.

FEMALE VOICE: No, Maxie. (*A slap is heard.*) Ow, that was sore. (*Voices of the two begin to drop.*)

JULIA: (*draws close to the wall and shouts*) Louder! I can't hear a thing. Come on, you can't start a story and then switch off the sound right in the middle. But I have, right here, my microphonic, amplifier stethoscope.

Takes out two acoustic implements, sticks them to the wall, pulls the wires across to the amplifier and inserts the pins into the machine. Instantly the voices of the two neighbours, still squabbling, can be heard clearly.

FEMALE VOICE: I know, Maxie . . . it's just that when I see you near another woman . . . I start thinking that you might be . . . you know what I mean . . . might be saying or doing to her what you say to me . . . oh, Maxie, I go out of my mind . . . I feel my legs shaking.

MALE VOICE: Come on, how could you imagine that I could ever prefer that hag to you . . . her bum hangs down round her ankles . . . Have you ever seen yourself next to her. In comparison to her, your bum looks as though it were tucked under your arms!

JULIA: A flamingo!

FEMALE VOICE: Ah, so it's just a question of bums?

MALE VOICE: No, no . . . eyes as well.

FEMALE VOICE: You mean my eyes are tucked under my arms?

MALE VOICE: Don't talk stupid . . . apart from the fact that I've always believed that a high bum means high emotions . . . there's no one on your level . . . I love you.

FEMALE VOICE: Yes, no one, no one . . . Go on, say it, Maxie.

MALE VOICE: No one can come up to you . . . not even in high heels. (*Little groans and kissing sounds.*)

JULIA: Better than *Dallas* any day!

MALE VOICE: I'm mad about you.

FEMALE VOICE: Again, again . . . say it again. Oh Maxie, you're wonderful. You're great . . . I'd die for love of you . . .

MALE VOICE: But you must promise that there will be no more of these scenes.

FEMALE VOICE: I promise. I promise.

MALE VOICE: And that you'll stop throwing these bronze book ends at my head.

FEMALE VOICE: No, never again at your head. No, darling, not like that. You're ripping my blouse. Let me.

MALE VOICE: No, let me. I enjoy it. God, what a lot of buttons.

FEMALE VOICE: I sewed on some extra ones just to tease you. Let me take your clothes off.

JULIA: Off! Off! Off!

MALE VOICE: You're a pet. Ahh . . . Ohh . . . like that. You take them off. Oww!

FEMALE VOICE: What's wrong, what have I done?

MALE VOICE: The zip, the zip in my trousers . . . it's caught the, the whatdyecallit . . . AAAh . . . it's sunk right in.

FEMALE VOICE: Oh, poor darling . . . wait and I'll fix it . . . oh my God, right on the tender spot. I can't move it.

MALE VOICE: Easy, easy. You're making it worse . . . Aaah help.

FEMALE VOICE: I'll have to cut off the trousers.

MALE VOICE: You'll do bugger all of the kind. They're brand new. Maybe we should go to the hospital. Aaaaah . . .

FEMALE VOICE: There you are. It's all done. Poor thing, I've cut a wee bit off.

MALE VOICE: You've what?

FEMALE VOICE: Come here and I'll look after you . . . a teensy weensy bandage . . .

ENGINEER'S VOICE: Bloody marvellous. You need the bandage yourself and you know where you can stick it. Use a whole roll. For God's sake! Are you going to give over with that wailing like a cat on heat. We're all needing a bit of sleep.

JULIA: That must be the engineer in Flat 3A.

PIANIST'S VOICE: Shut up, you dirty old bastard, you! Leave these two young people who love each other alone. They're so sweet.

JULIA: The pianist woman in 3B! (*The two lovers fall silent.*) There, I knew it, complete silence. So I'll never know if love is stronger than the bandage. (*The chicken is cooked. JULIA removes it from the pot, places it on a serving dish, garnishes it with olives, a slice of orange, and lettuce leaves. Looks at her handiwork and says.*) Lovely, but just the same you make me sick. You're nothing but a clapped out battery hen. Every day stuck in there with thousands of others, and a pair of green glasses over your beak to make you believe that the garbage you were gobbling up was top quality lettuce and fresh peas! Bloody idiot! And am I supposed to munch my way through a corpse like that? The last meal of the condemned prisoner? Not bloody likely. I'd rather die with an empty stomach. You sleep the eternal sleep more peacefully that way. No fear of nightmares. (*Goes to sit down, looks around her, heaves a sigh.*)

I'll need to find a way of finishing this commercial. I could make him watch the last preparations. Slowly, slowly, take out the bottle, the syringe, do the injection and then, slowly, the death mask. (*Makes a sickly grin.*) No, poor boy, he'd never get to sleep again.

For a few seconds she gazes around her silently, not sure what to do next. Her eyes fall on the magazine Health. *She picks it up, and reads, section by section, the article in question.*

'A warm brick under your back level with your kidneys . . . the head hanging over the side . . . humming vowel sounds.' I must have a go. Why not? I've tried everything else. Right then, first thing, the brick. How about the lid of the chicken pot. (*Picks up the lid.*) Still hot. Prepare the table. (*Removes the tablecloth and plates. Places the lid on the table. Lies down on top.*) Please God don't let me levitate too high. (*Lies down. Begins to wail.*) Ahaa . . . Ooooh I see where the sounds come from. (*Lets her head hang over the edge of the table, starts the humming effect.*) AUoooo . . . Aiiooo . . . it's all in the mind, but I do feel relaxed. Aooeee . . . Auooiieeuuoooh.

ENGINEER'S VOICE: At it again are we? Back to the cat on the tiles routine, eh?

PIANIST'S VOICE: On you go, groan away. Pay no heed to that decrepit old so and so. (*The* PIANIST *encourages them by playing the piano. The two lovers in the next room start breathing heavily once again.*)

FEMALE VOICE: Yes, yes . . . oh Maxie . . . I could die . . .

MALE VOICE: Easy now . . . Ouch. You're knocking off the bandage.

FEMALE VOICE: Oh, how lovely. Aah . . . I'll put it back on in a minute. I'll put on a whole roll of gauze. Oh God! Oh God!

MALE VOICE: Oh God, you're killing me.

JULIA: I always wonder why when people are making love, God always gets mixed with it. Oh God, how lovely! Oh God, I could die!

FEMALE VOICE: More, more! Oh Mother of God, I can't take any more.

JULIA: Every so often, you get God's Holy Mother as well.

PIANIST'S VOICE: Oh yes, more . . . go on, more, more.

ENGINEER'S VOICE: For God's sake, stop.

From outside the sound of a baby crying.

JULIA: Already! A bouncing baby boy! The child of the bandage! (*Comes down from the table, saying.*) I'm starving. (*Looks at the chicken.*) I'm not touching you. Right into the bin with you. What can I have? (*Clapping her hands.*) Spaghetti, the first recorded case of spaghetti suicide. Let's really go to town, one quarter, a half pound, three quarters of a pound of spaghetti . . . an overdose of pasta. Fill up the pot with water (*Putting in the water.*) and I'll swallow one of these little pills to reduce animal fat. (*Places the pot on a gas ring.*) Spaghetti . . . spaghetti. (*The phone rings and* JULIA *lifts the receiver.*) Hello!

KATIE'S VOICE (*on telephone*): Doctor, please, please don't start shouting at me. I really must talk to you . . . hello, can you hear me?

JULIA: Hello. Yes, I'm listening.

KATIE'S VOICE: It is you, right. You are the doctor. I haven't got the wrong number.

JULIA: (*with resignation*) No, you haven't. It's me, the analyst. (*To herself.*) Why not?

KATIE'S VOICE: Perhaps I've chosen an awkward time to call.

JULIA: Well, in fact, it is just a bit inconvenient.

KATIE'S VOICE: I could ring you back later, if you're still up.

JULIA: That's just it. Later on I won't be . . . up.

KATIE'S VOICE: Is there something wrong, Doctor? From your voice, you sound a bit down.

JULIA: No, no, I'm fine . . . just a bit tired, you know how it is. Unfortunately, not all of my patients who call me at home are civil and understanding, like you. There's one who has the little problem of waiting for the blue window . . . then there's one who bites the balls off a client . . . and . . .

KATIE'S VOICE: They chewed the balls off one of your clients, in one go!

JULIA: No, the client wasn't mine. Anyway it's a long story, too long for the moment. Let's forget it. Tell me all about yourself. Hang on a minute till I change the receiver. (*Pulls out the plug from the wall and puts it into a machine linked to a headset of the type used by exchange-operators.*) Sorry, but I was just sitting down to eat.

KATIE'S VOICE: Forgive me. I know I am being a nuisance.

JULIA: Don't worry, with this headset I can move about quite freely.

KATIE'S VOICE: A headset?

JULIA: I had to get one a while back for when my mother phones up. She goes on and on for hours. I used to be stuck there listening to her. This way I can listen to her and go about my business. So, you were saying.

KATIE'S VOICE: (*aggressively*) Yes, well, I have tried out your method and pardon me if I'm quite frank with you, but the only result was that while I was warbling away, the firemen and the police came storming up.

JULIA: (*laughs*) Ha! Ha! . . . Really.

KATIE'S VOICE: (*annoyed*) I am glad you find it so funny.

JULIA: I didn't mean to laugh at you . . . you've got a good sense of humour yourself . . . So you mean to say you got no benefit at all from the . . . course of treatment.

KATIE'S VOICE: Quite the reverse. I could have kicked myself.

JULIA: Why?

KATIE'S VOICE: Oh, come on. A woman of my age, with a brick under her bum and her head see-sawing back and forward . . . it's not real. I don't know how I could have fallen for such gibberish.

JULIA: (*amused but making an effort to appear offended*) Gibberish! A method tried and tested in Japan.

KATIE'S VOICE: That's just it. You had to go to Japan to try it out, because if you had done your experiments here, they'd have knocked you black and blue and tossed you in the clink for a bloody fraud.

JULIA: Oh so that's it! Black and blue, eh. You come on to my phone, in my home, just to insult me, right at the very moment . . . you have no idea how delicate this moment is for me . . . and all this to tell me I should be knocked black and blue and tossed into the slammer. There's no end of people who want to see you drown in the shit. I was better off with my street-walker. All she wanted to do was to burn down my house and bite off my husband's whatnots . . .

KATIE'S VOICE: Take it easy . . . I'm sorry, you're quite right. I'm an aggressive, loud-mouthed, ill-tempered cow.

JULIA: (*during this conversation she is setting the table and putting the spaghetti in the pot*) Now hold on . . .

KATIE'S VOICE: Self-centred and feeble-minded.

JULIA: Don't overdo it.

KATIE'S VOICE: A right bitch.

JULIA: Oh well, if you insist.

KATIE'S VOICE: It's just that I'm going through a bad patch. If only you knew, Doctor.

JULIA: You don't need to tell me.

KATIE'S VOICE: I cannot stand anything or anybody. Look, I wasn't always so gloomy and aggressive.

JULIA: Yes, but, these are the classic symptoms of paranoia, the very ones I've got myself, by the way . . . You spend all day observing your own navel as though it was the centre of the world. You let a little tear splash into your navel every so often till it forms a tiny pool, and then you dip in your finger and shout . . . 'Look, the ocean'.

KATIE'S VOICE: You dip in your finger and say that it is the ocean!

JULIA: Metaphorically. It was a literary paradox.

KATIE'S VOICE: Thank God for that!

JULIA: (*puts her hand over the microphone receiver, says to herself*) Here, it's not bad this business of being an analyst. I have found a vocation. A pity it's too late.

KATIE'S VOICE: Anyway I wanted to let you know that you have got the wrong person. If you wanted somebody to make a fool of themselves, I am myself the number one. If you came to my house, you could have a look at the posters hanging on my walls.

JULIA: You've got posters on your walls. What do they say?

KATIE'S VOICE: Well, for instance, I am trying to kick smoking and to lose weight.

JULIA: Not another one.

KATIE'S VOICE: Why? Are you reducing or are you worried about smoking?

JULIA: Who isn't? Women doctors get fat as well, you know.

KATIE'S VOICE: Yes, of course. And to think that just today I was going to get stuck into a whole chicken. It nearly made me spew.

JULIA: Don't tell me. So you chucked it out.

KATIE'S VOICE: No, I wrapped it up in a nice little package and posted it off to my landlady. She wants to evict me. With a bit of luck, and with the way the post works nowadays, it'll be stinking to high heaven when she gets it.

JULIA: (*laughing*) Ha! Ha! Very naughty of you, but I like your style.

KATIE'S VOICE: Style . . . Yeah . . . enough style to make you sick. I have one hell of a neurosis that I just cannot get over. My body is scarcely in working order, I eat raw grain and I stick garlic suppositories up my bum so I end up with breath like a dragon in a zoo.

JULIA: Listen, I must tell you something, and I am not speaking as a psychiatrist. In fact, I may as well tell you that I am an ordinary woman, somebody that you got on the phone by mistake. And the incredible thing is that you seem to be a photocopy of me. It is as though I was looking at myself in a huge mirror. You see, I feel empty and desperate, just the same as you, and perhaps even more. I go around hanging up posters and I eat the right food and what's more I believe I am an emancipated, modern woman just because I have electrical and electronic gadgets, even in the toilet.

KATIE'S VOICE: Stop right there, Doctor. I know where you are heading. I am not one of your half-witted ravers that you lead by the nose with this guff about mirror games or by yelling 'Same here! Same here!'

JULIA: So you don't believe me. You think I'm a phoney.

KATIE'S VOICE: Quite the reverse. I think that you are one of the best. Thank God that you are neither a psychiatrist nor one of these trendy analysts.

JULIA: What do you mean I'm not an anal . . .

KATIE'S VOICE: (*interrupting*) I understood after we had been talking for five seconds. Your language is too human and intelligent for you to belong to my profession.

JULIA: Your profession? You mean you are . . . ?

KATIE'S VOICE: Yes, I am a doctor.

JULIA: Why didn't you tell me to shut up earlier?

KATIE'S VOICE: Because I really needed someone like you . . . someone to talk about ordinary, everyday things . . . before I kick the bucket.

JULIA: Kick the bucket! What are you up to?

KATIE'S VOICE: I am going quietly. Can you still hear me? I am finding it hard to get the words out.

JULIA: What have you done, Doctor? Speak. Have you taken something?

KATIE'S VOICE: No, I've switched on the gas . . . very slightly . . . so that I can go almost without noticing. You know, it is quite a pleasing feeling.

JULIA: Listen, this time you have got to believe me. This is not a trick. I had decided to finish myself off as well. I have already got a solution of paraquat all ready, you know that weedkiller stuff. I was going to take it in a wee while.

KATIE'S VOICE: No kidding! What a coincidence.

JULIA: Do you not believe me?

KATIE'S VOICE: Yeah, I believe you. Oh well, then, all the best.

JULIA: No, wait a minute. I had my mind made up until a few minutes ago, then this carry on of acting the analyst, of listening to other people's despair, of hearing the very words that I think and say but speak with a different voice . . . Well, it all seemed so absurd! First it was all so logical, and now it just seems madness.

KATIE'S VOICE: Well, you know what they say, madness and logic are so near.

JULIA: Come on now, tell me where you live. Give me your address and I'll come round, we can talk . . .

KATIE'S VOICE: We've done enough talking, don't you think, and it was really nice. I really needed to hear a kindly voice like yours to keep me company as I slip away.

JULIA: Please, I beg you. Give me this chance. Tell me where you live.

KATIE'S VOICE: I really am so grateful for your concern, but it is no use. Quite apart from the fact that it would be dangerous for you, because I have been fixing up the wires of the doorbell so that the first person who presses the button sets off a spark and BOOM, the whole place'll be up in the air. I don't want those bastards of my relatives to find even the teeniest piece of furniture or the slightest rag of my clothes to divide among themselves. And I'd give anything to see the face of the landlady who threw me out. 'Go on, let's see you renting out this heap now!' Anyway enough of this. I have been intruding on your courtesy too long.

JULIA: Hold on, don't hang up. Try and be reasonable!

KATIE'S VOICE: Reasonable? Now that's rich. Listen to who's talking. You have decided to do away with yourself with paraquat weedkiller, and you tell me to be reasonable. (*A ring from the buzzer.*)

JULIA: Just a minute, don't go away. There's somebody at the door. I'll be right back.

KATIE'S VOICE: OK, I'll hold on, but not for long.

JULIA: (*runs over to the intercom*) Hello.

DOORKEEPER'S VOICE: It's the doorkeeper. There are two delivery men with flowers for you. I'll just send them up.

JULIA: No, wait, hello. Hold them there and I'll . . . hello. She's hung up. (*Re-adjusts the headset.*) Hello, Doctor. Still there. Can you hear me?

KATIE'S VOICE: Yes . . . I can hear you . . . Your voice has gone funny . . . it's starting to work.

JULIA: Pay attention to this. Throw the windows wide open. Switch off the gas. At least tell me your name.

KATIE'S VOICE: What's the point? Anyway, if you really must . . . I'm called Katie.

JULIA: Listen to me, Katie, if you have decided to kill yourself, nobody is going to pay any heed.

KATIE'S VOICE: Maybe not . . . but right now I have the guts it takes . . . I can do it . . . afterwards who knows?

JULIA: But don't you have a voice telling you that perhaps it is not guts at all, but cowardice. I'm saying this to you because . . . (*A ring at the door.* JULIA, *still talking, goes towards the outside door.*) it might be the fear of facing up to . . . (*Loudly towards the door.*) I'm coming . . . (*Talking into the telephone again.*) the terror of (*Opens the door. A huge bouquet of flowers is literally hurled into her face.*) . . . My God! (*The telephone headset is knocked off. Two men, one young, the other older, appear from behind the flowers. They have guns pointed at* JULIA.)

OLDER MAN: Freeze! If you move or scream, you're dead.

YOUNG MAN: It's a hold-up. And blowing you to smithereens won't bother us.

JULIA: Pity. If you had got here a wee while ago, you would have done me a good turn.

OLDER MAN: What are you on about? Don't get scared. We are not staying, but we want your cash, the lot.

JULIA: Bad luck, lads. I was just setting off, shall we say, on my travels.

YOUNG MAN: Fine. Hand over your travelling money.

JULIA: It was a free trip . . . One way.

OLDER MAN: Listen here, no more messing about, understand? Fish out all that you've got, otherwise . . .

JULIA: Cool it, now, take it easy. No problem. You can have the lot, OK? (*Goes for her handbag.*)

YOUNG MAN: (*grabs the bag*) Not so fast!

JULIA: There's only seven pounds.

YOUNG MAN: Bloody hell. She's right. One fiver and two singles.

OLDER MAN: You wouldn't like to get us all wound up, now would you? Get the dough out, like I said.

He lifts the cigarette lighter to threaten JULIA. *Sets off the mechanism, the pictures open out, the siren goes off and the light starts flashing.*

YOUNG MAN: Oh Christ. The alarm. (*Rushes towards the exit.*)

OLDER MAN: Stop there. It's just posters and pictures arsing about.

JULIA: Yes, it's just my little game. It's a trap I invented for myself to force me to stop smoking.

YOUNG MAN: Bitch! You've got me all trembling. (*Gives her a slap. The lights go out.*) What's going on now?

JULIA: When you hit me, you made the transformer blow.

YOUNG MAN: When I hit you!

JULIA: That's right. You see that box on the wall? It's a sensor which goes on and off every time it hears a smack. Allow me. (*Gives him an almighty slap. The light goes back on.*)

YOUNG MAN: Hey! What are you at?

JULIA: There you see. It works.

YOUNG MAN: Yes but, you bastard. I'll blow your head off. (*Points the gun.*)

OLDER MAN: (*stops him with a blow. Lights go off*) Cut it out, you idiot. (*Another slap to bring the lights back.*) If you kill her, who's going to tell us where the loot is, eh? (*Another punch.*)

YOUNG MAN: Don't you go punching me . . . and don't call me an idiot, OK? (*Gives him a punch. Light effect. They hit each other, with the lights going on and off.*)

JULIA: Have you finished? Don't overdo this one potato, two potato act, boys, you'll break the switch. Why don't you get on with this hold-up? Take what you fancy and get on your way because I've got some important business to attend to. (*Picks up the telephone headset.*)

OLDER MAN: Just what is that?

JULIA: It is a telephonist's headset. When you came in with the flowers I was chatting to a friend.

OLDER MAN: A friend. So this woman must have heard everything. Give here. (*Puts the ear piece to his ear.*) She's hung up.

JULIA: Oh God!

YOUNG MAN: She must have phoned the police.

JULIA: Not at all. The way she was feeling.

YOUNG MAN: Do you see her game now? The bitch! That's why she was clowning about . . . to gain time. Let's get out of here. (*Goes towards door but is stopped by his companion.*)

OLDER MAN: Not so fast!

YOUNG MAN: The police'll be here any minute. (*Tries to pull himself free, but receives a punch. Lights off.*)

OLDER MAN: We're not leaving empty handed, do you understand?

Deals the younger man a blow, at which he grabs a bottle from the trolley intending to smash it over the head of his companion. The mechanism snaps into action. The written message comes up. The recorded voice booms out. Terrified, the younger man drops the bottle.

PEREMPTORY VOICE: It's no good kidding yourself on! There's no way out!

OLDER MAN: What the hell's that?

YOUNG MAN: They've got us. (*Makes to run for it.*)

PEREMPTORY VOICE: Alcohol kills slowly but inexorably.

JULIA: (*grabs the bottle, puts it back on the trolley. Silence falls, everything goes back into its place. Slowly*) Another of my little tricks to make me cut down on alcohol.

OLDER MAN: If you don't quit buggering us about . . .

Aims another blow, but this time JULIA *bends down and the blow lands on the* YOUNG MAN's *face. Lights off.*

JULIA: No more violence against women! (*Throws a tremendous punch and the robber falls to the ground. Lights on.*)

YOUNG MAN: Get a move on. The police are on the way.

OLDER MAN: The dough, fast.

JULIA: But I have no more, I swear it. I wasn't expecting you.

YOUNG MAN: The jewels will do, starting with these ones. (*Seizes the necklace* JULIA *has round her neck. All the pearls clatter to the ground.*

OLDER MAN: You bloody idiot! (*Blow. Lights off.*) When did you ever see anyone in the pictures grabbing necklaces like that? Put on the light. (*The* YOUNG MAN *slaps himself on the face and the lights come back on.*) It'll take at least half an hour to pick them up one by one.

JULIA: If I were you, I wouldn't waste my time . . . I picked it up at a jumble sale, it is not worth much. (*The younger robber, fiddling about with the video-tape, has switched on the camera.*) Please, don't touch. These are very sensitive machines. If you are desperate to tape your partner, allow me. Wouldn't you like to come on screen too. Big smile. 'Real life hold-up of a woman on her own with punch-up and special lighting effects.'

OLDER MAN: Hey, cut that out. (*To the younger man.*) You've been high on drugs so long, your brain's clapped out. What do you think you're doing? Why don't you run along with your cassette to your nearest police station? (*To JULIA.*) Turn off this trap and rub out the tape.

YOUNG MAN: It's you that's off your head. And quit calling me crazy or I'll go mad. You think this machine is a trap . . . You're still after jewellery . . . How much do you think this little baby is worth, eh? At least £5000. (*To JULIA.*) Isn't that right? Come on, how much did it cost you? Speak, you bitch.

JULIA: Now, come on, fair's fair . . . You're not really . . . I need this for my work. If you take it away, how am I going to live?

OLDER MAN: What do you care? You're going off on your travels, aren't you? (*The two start loading the camera and the video-recorder on their backs.*)

JULIA: At least leave me that one cassette, because I have recorded . . .

YOUNG MAN: We'll not be long in rubbing it off. Don't you worry.

OLDER MAN: Get a hold of that radio.

JULIA: Nooo! Not the radio.

OLDER MAN: (*to JULIA, brandishing his gun*) You stay nice and quiet. I'm warning you, if you call anybody, I'll be right back to blow your brains out.

JULIA: No, no, cool it. (*The two struggle out with their burden.*) Let me get the door . . . good-bye, I mean good evening. (*The two go out. JULIA closes the door behind them and puts the headset back on.*) Hello, Katie. Damn, she really has hung up. (*Takes off the headset.*) What do I do now? God, that bastard really hit me. (*Pulls herself together.*) The police! Must call right away. What's the number? What a fool, 999, just as well I know it off by heart. (*Dials the number*.) It's ringing. Hurry up. There they are. Hello.

POLICEMAN'S VOICE (*on telephone*): Hello, police station here.

JULIA: Sorry I am finding it hard to get the words out. He gave me such a thump that he left me reeling.

POLICEMAN'S VOICE: Who did, madam?

JULIA: A burglar, two burglars in fact.

POLICEMAN'S VOICE: You've been burgled, madam? When was this?

JULIA: Yes, just two minutes ago . . . at my house . . . they came in with flowers . . . but this is not why I am phoning . . . it's that . . .

POLICEMAN'S VOICE: Where do you live?

JULIA: 138 Bentinck Street, fourth floor, second door right . . . but it is urgent that you go to . . .

POLICEMAN'S VOICE: 138 Bentinck Street, fourth floor, second on right, telephone number 611 3002.

JULIA: How did you know?

POLICEMAN'S VOICE: A woman phoned up a short time ago to report a burglary at that address.

JULIA: Good. That's the woman you've got to trace at once. Did she leave her address?

POLICEMAN'S VOICE: That's the problem. We asked her but she refused. We thought we were dealing with a hoaxer. Her voice sounded unnatural, as though she were drunk.

JULIA: No, she's not drunk. She's on gas.

POLICEMAN'S VOICE: Grass?

JULIA: Not grass, she's not on drugs. She's switched on the gas. Now you'll need to be very careful when you ring the bell . . . that is under no circumstances ring the bell, because she has criss-crossed the wires, so that the whole place will blow up.

POLICEMAN'S VOICE: What will blow up?

JULIA: The flat, with the furniture and everything . . . because she does not want to leave even the teeniest stick to those bastards of relatives of hers . . . and the landlady will be left trying to rent out the rubble . . . you understand? But do not waste time, get round there, because if you don't, she's as good as dead.

POLICEMAN'S VOICE: OK, we're on our way. Would you be good enough to give us the address?

JULIA: I don't know it.

POLICEMAN'S VOICE: You mean to tell me you don't know where your gassy friend lives.

JULIA: Well it's not like that. I only met her this evening, because of the magazine *Health*, you see they published my number instead of the Japanese analyst's.

POLICEMAN'S VOICE: Japanese analyst?

JULIA: Yes, but my crazy friend isn't the only one who got it wrong . . . just imagine there was a woman who asked if it was all right to put a warm brick on her bum even although the window wasn't blue . . .

POLICEMAN'S VOICE: Just take it easy, madam.

JULIA: I am taking it easy. I'd like to see you in my place. Here was I making my going away video, as calm as you like . . . because I was going to commit suicide with paraquat weedkiller, when those women started phoning. Hello, Doctor, you'd better be a psychiatrist, if not I'm coming round to burn down your house . . . and we'll have a shoot-out, like *High Noon*. BANG BANG . . . because I am so overwrought, and I have bitten off a testicle from one of my clients and it rolled like a little ball under the cupboard and I'm carrying it around in an ice bag and the people at the hospital will sew it on right away.

POLICEMAN'S VOICE: Let's get this straight, madam, did I hear you say that you bit off a ball belonging to one of your clients?

JULIA: No, not me, for goodness' sake. I'm a vegetarian. But you're getting me confused. We've got to find out where my friend lives!

POLICEMAN'S VOICE: Quite so. Could you at least tell us her name?

JULIA: Silly me. It's coming back to me now – she's called Katie.

POLICEMAN'S VOICE: Uh huh. Katie. Surname?

JULIA: I don't know. She didn't tell me. But she did say that she is a doctor.

POLICEMAN'S VOICE: That's a start. Now try hard to recall any other detail that may have emerged during the conversation.

JULIA: Yes, well, she said that she was following her jockey's diet and that she is trying to give up smoking.

POLICEMAN'S VOICE: Not a great deal of help, but carry on.

JULIA: She's another one who puts up terrorist posters on the wall.

POLICEMAN'S VOICE: Terrorist posters?

JULIA: That's right. She does mad things. She boils the chicken then doesn't eat it.

POLICEMAN'S VOICE: If she doesn't eat it, what does she do with it?

JULIA: She throws it out. No, no, as you were. It's me that throws it out. She puts it in the post, so that it is rotten and stinking when it gets to the landlady.

POLICEMAN'S VOICE: That is an interesting detail.

JULIA: Maybe I am going on a bit, but I assure you that the story is really tragic.

POLICEMAN'S VOICE: Madam, put yourself in my place. What would you think of somebody who phones you up to tell you that she is going to kill herself, but won't tell you where she lives?

JULIA: But she didn't tell me right away that she was going to kill herself. At the beginning, she just wanted a wee chat with another human being, not with a doctor.

POLICEMAN'S VOICE: And in the course of talking to you, she decided to gas herself!

JULIA: She had already made up her mind . . . same as me, so that's why, as I was just telling you, I was having a quiet chat with my husband, who's not here, because we don't live together any more . . . Maybe I still love him, even if I tell him I don't, so he doesn't go around preening himself like the cock of the north. Well then, she, this gassy friend of mine, needled me a bit, in fact she actually insulted me . . . 'What do you mean scorching your clients on the bum' says she 'and forcing them to make humming sounds AIUA OOO.' Do you follow?

POLICEMAN'S VOICE: Couldn't be clearer.

JULIA: So, says she . . . I start humming the notes and what happens? The firemen come rushing in, the cats start miaowing and the neighbours are at it through the wall. No, the bit about the neighbours was me.

POLICEMAN'S VOICE: You don't say.

JULIA: Listen, I have the distinct impression that you are taking the mickey.

POLICEMAN'S VOICE: God forbid!

JULIA: Do you not realise that time is short and that poor woman is dying? What's keeping you back? There's all this claptrap on the telly about your data banks that can track down your criminals in a flash, but when it comes to saving some poor unfortunate that is gassing herself . . .

POLICEMAN'S VOICE: Stay calm, very calm. By the way, what did you say your name was?

JULIA: What have I got to do with it? It's not me that needs to be saved . . .

POLICEMAN'S VOICE: I'm not so sure about that.

JULIA: Take my word for it, I am all right now . . . all because of her, this Katie . . . she was like a mirror for me . . . a huge mirror . . . that gave a grotesque reflection . . . and everything became clear. She was talking the same language as me . . . An absurd photocopy. It was like being hit by lightning. All of a sudden I caught a glimpse of myself, and I looked . . . funny . . . like nothing on earth. These are the right words, funny and like nothing on earth. I saw my own madness, do you understand me, as though finally projected in the right frame. Here you are, I said to myself, I am down a bit but why am I staring at my navel and dipping my fingers in with the tears? Let's just stop shouting . . . God bless the ocean! I am going to stop staying all by myself at home with these electronic gadgets and traps and diets . . . oh my God, the spaghetti! It'll be all stuck together. But who cares? Do you know, it has just occurred to me, all of a sudden, that in next to no time it's going to be spring. Hello, hello! Anybody there? He's hung up on me. Must be crazy or something. Maybe we were cut off. (*Starts ringing the number, hears a buzz from the intercom, goes to answer*.) Hello, what's going on?

DOORKEEPER'S VOICE: There is an ambulance here with some nurses. They're wanting to know if it was you that was burgled.

JULIA: Yes, it was me, but what's the ambulance for? I'm not injured, just a wee bit dazed from the punches.

DOORKEEPER'S VOICE: Sorry, there's a doctor here and he wants to talk to you personally.

JULIA: What doctor?

DOCTOR'S VOICE: Good evening. Now don't get excited. We're coming up right away.

JULIA: Wait a minute. There's been some mistake. Are you a doctor?

DOCTOR'S VOICE: They phoned us from the police station. We're on our way up. Open the door will you? Can you walk by yourself?

JULIA: What do you mean?

DOCTOR'S VOICE: Just what I say. Can you walk unaided? If not, we'll bring the stretcher.

JULIA: The stretcher? Hold it right there!

DOCTOR'S VOICE: Another thing. Be a good girl, take the wire from the bell. Isolate it, would you. We are not going to press the bell, but you can't be too careful . . . and, open the windows wide, if you can manage.

JULIA: No . . . You've got it all mixed up . . . it was the other woman who was on the gas . . . I was the one with the paraquat . . .

DOCTOR'S VOICE: And the weedkiller. I know, I know. The lads at the station told us all about it . . . the chicken stinking to high heaven slipped in the post box, the balls bit off in ice, and the blue window. Don't worry about a thing, we're coming, just relax and do not put up any resistance.

JULIA: What resistance could I put up? What do you want to do to me? Do you think I'm mad? I'm not going to any asylum.

VOICE AT THE DOOR: Now, open up or we'll have to knock the door down.

JULIA: (*in despair*) No, not the asylum . . . I'm not going to any asylum, no, no, no asylum . . .

Lights go down slowly as the music comes up.